Advance Pra

FORGIVING ALL MY LIVES

"Barret Hedeen is a gifted healer and consummate teacher of *A Course in Miracles*. His journey of awakening through forgiveness of his past lives is fascinating and instructive to both students of the Course and any other spiritual path. This book has the capacity to accelerate spiritual awakening when it is read and absorbed. This book is a gift to the world!"
~ LORRI COBURN, author of *Breaking Free: How Forgiveness and A Course in Miracles Can Set You Free*

"Forgiving All My Lives is overflowing with pure love, fresh insights, and exercises you can try for yourself. Barret Hedeen's exploration of past lives, using the forgiveness practice from *A Course in Miracles*, opens the door to profound, multi-level healing. His stories inspire the reader to trust your vulnerability and open to what seems impossible. Read it once for pleasure, and then again to exorcise your own demons once and for all." ~ AMY TORRES, author of *Sweet Dreams of Awakening*

"This book is a beautiful journey into deep healing. It will open your mind to the many opportunities we have to release the past and experience the truth in this present moment. I am struck by Barret's willingness to allow whatever is coming up in his experience to rise and be healed. We can all learn from his example."
~ CORINNE ZUPKO, award-winning author of *From Anxiety To Love*

"Barret does a great job in bringing together the healing of past lifetimes and *A Course in Miracles*. This book is humorous, authentic, and right on point!" ~ MARIA FELIPE, author of *Live Your Happy!*

"Forgiving All My Lives is like a glass of fresh water. Barret weaves a story with such delicate insights that you feel like you are taking the road to enlightenment with a good friend, who is kind enough to show you all the bumpy parts and short cuts. Returning to love never looked so easy." ~ MAUREEN MULDOON, author of *The Spiritual Vixen's Guide to an Unapologetic Life*

"With this beautiful book, Barret Hedeen gives us a concise, practical, and very useful explanation of how to break the ego's cycle of karma and set your path firmly home to God. I was both impressed and entertained. I highly recommend this enlightening book!" ~ GARY RENARD, best-selling author of *The Disappearance of the Universe* trilogy and *The Lifetimes When Jesus and Buddha Knew Each Other*

Forgiving *All My Lives*

Clearing Karma with
A Course in Miracles

❧

Barret Hedeen

© Copyright 2020 by
Barret Hedeen
https://BarretHedeen.com/
Contact: *Barret@BarretHedeen.com*
City of Publication: Milwaukee, WI

ISBN: 979-8-64095-260-5

Library of Congress Control Number:
2020908540

All quotes are from *A Course in Miracles,* Third Edition,
published in 2007, by the Foundation for Inner Peace,
448 Ignacio Blvd. #306, Novato CA 94949.
www.acim.org

This book was produced in collaboration with Fearless Literary,
which represents all subsidiary rights. For more information,
write *info@fearlessbooks.com.*

DESIGN & TYPOGRAPHY:
Fearless Literary Services
www.fearlessbooks.com

TABLE OF CONTENTS

To Ken:

Your lightness and joy echo throughout time and space, beckoning us beyond them to the Oneness we all truly are.

Acknowledgments

I feel very grateful to be sharing this book with the world. As grateful as I am to be getting it into the hands of you, the reader, I am perhaps even more grateful for all of the beautiful connections that it has facilitated in my life. What a real blessing this writing and publishing journey has been!

Deep thanks to all of my friends and family who have supported me with their kindness and their love. Mom, Dad, Kay, Nikki, Justus, Katie, Dave and Xavier — I love you guys all so much! Thank you, Edith, for all your support throughout the years.

I have been blessed with two amazing book birthers/editors extraordinaire. Tammy Letherer, our editing sessions cleared out the roughest pieces of my raw manuscript, while simultaneously being kind and profoundly sweet. D. Patrick Miller, your finely-honed wordsmithing abilities brought my writings to a whole 'nother level. I am deeply indebted to you both.

The number of wonderful healers I've worked with over the years has been an astounding gift to me – many of whom are dear friends as well! Cindy Libman, Dan Hanneman, E. Jason Gremley, Paula Battaglio, Sharon Berkowitz, Melissa Matson, Cheryl Good, Lorri Coburn, Jenny Donner, Diamond Haracz, Laurra Warnke, Jeneen Stickney, Bhairavi Shera, Paul Zavagno, Carla Starla, Gale West, Shakta Kaur, Kate Krizka, kironJ Gardner, Charlie Roberts, Preston Klik, Barry Kerr, Christine Gay, Emily Klik. Thank you, thank you, thank you!

There are so many wonderful teachers in the *A Course in Miracles* community to appreciate, that I will just name the two I come back to again and again for the incredible consistency, clarity and compassion in their teachings. Ken Wapnick, you have pointed me unerringly to look at the cause (the mistaken belief in separation) instead of getting mired in the effect of the world of time and space. My endless gratitude to you and your Foundation for *A Course in Miracles*. And Gary Renard, who I told along with his wife Cindy after a workshop they had led, "Your teaching does honor to the author of the Course! Thank you so much!"

INTRODUCTION

Hearing the Call for Love

I am not a body. I am free. For I am still as God created me.
—A COURSE IN MIRACLES

I CAN FEEL these words resonating through my mind — comforting, reassuring, yet also terrifying. Part of me wants to let go into the joy, the perfect bliss, the oneness of the real Divine. Yet I also want to run away and settle myself into a big bag of chips or cookies — anything to take my mind off the subtle, yet overwhelming sense of terror this thought evokes. How can I be perfect Truth, beyond form, beyond symbol? This body sure seems like my home. After all, I've experienced it this way every day for over forty years. This push-pull within me has become familiar since the day, fourteen years ago, when I began studying *A Course in Miracles.*

In early 2001, my life was going through some turmoil. I guess you could say I was trying to find myself. After graduating from Northwestern University with a degree in Computer Science the previous June, I dove into an attempt to change the world. I had been accepted into Teach For America, a program that matches non-Education major college graduates with schools in need of teachers. I made it through the summer training program, but dropped out before the school year got under way. I was placed to teach a sixth-grade special education classroom, and I was in way over my head. Feeling frozen and overwhelmed, I resigned from the program. I was ashamed; I had never quit anything so big. Moving back to Wisconsin to live at home with my mother felt like a major setback, and I ended up struggling with depression.

In what seemed like a fortuitous turn of events, a friend of mine from college told me about the Landmark Forum. It had helped him to let go of much fear and move through his life with less anxiety and uncertainty. Depression was preventing any next step in my life, so I signed up for the weekend workshop after looking at the information online. Landmark's purpose, according to the promotional material, was to induce participants to have a transformational experience. But their techniques, which included discouraging participants from leaving their seats, late-night sessions, early starts, and a lot of homework, led to mild sleep deprivation and seemed to me to lack a certain amount of kindness and caring.

Still, I was soon 'all in' on Landmark and trying to convince everyone I knew to sign up. They actively encouraged recruiting, telling us "If this was such a good experience for you, why wouldn't you want to share this with your loved ones?" The spiritual and emotional pressure cooker of the process certainly resulted in a lot of breakthroughs for me. I was seeing and moving through layers of resistance within myself that I hadn't known were there. But I was unmoored and directionless, bouncing around like a pinball in all directions. I was frightening and upsetting my family members with some of the things I was saying to them. Within a couple of days, I realized that this program wasn't for me, and that my erratic behavior was not a helpful thing.

Soon after the weekend, I fell asleep in my car in a grocery store's parking lot. The car was running because it was cold outside, and I had just finished a bite to eat. I startled awake, and the first thing that came to my mind was a couple of people my mom had known who died of carbon monoxide poisoning sitting in their car while it ran on a winter day. The exhaust had backed up into their car, and they had fatally fallen asleep.

I went into a deep panic, thinking that I had almost accidentally killed myself, when it's likely there was no exhaust in the cabin of the car. I was just tired from not getting enough sleep. However, this panicked state didn't subside, and when I went into the grocery store, it was clear to the workers that I was in distress. I was so shaken, I was too upset to drive. A very kind manager reached out to my family and figured out what train I could take to get to them. He even walked me to the train station nearby, since I hadn't been on that train line before.

Fairly soon after that, my parents took me in to get some help, and we agreed that it would be best for me to stay in a psychiatric facility for a bit. I stayed there a few days and left on some mood-stabilizing medicines that were helpful to me for the next year and a half. It took me a while to put myself back together, but I didn't know exactly what that meant. The experience of deep inner opening, and becoming aware of old wounds through the Landmark process had clearly led to massive emotional shifts, and a deep desire had been activated within me to clear my inner landscape of old pains. I also knew that whatever paths I followed would have to be interwoven with compassion. Over the next several years, I was able to start integrating the shifts I had experienced, and do so in a way that felt loving and kind, not jarring and disjunctive.

The following year, after some trepidation and a questioning conversation with the facilitator, I signed up for an eight-week meditation course. I wanted to be sure that this experience wouldn't lead me to fall apart as I had done before. She assured me that there was no pressure applied with these techniques, just being consistent and gentle with the process of developing inner awareness and mental focus, in the form of mindfulness meditation. I decided to give it a try, knowing that I could leave the group if it ever felt like it was becoming too much for me.

The group turned out to be very helpful and instructive. I began practicing several different simple meditation techniques, feeling encouraged but not pressed to share my experiences with the group as we went forward. Most days, we were asked to listen to a guided meditation that had been recorded by the facilitator on CD. I was usually good at following directions, so I stuck to the practice closely.

After six or seven weeks, I had a turning point while meditating to one of the recordings she had given us. I was sitting on a pillow with my legs crossed, and feeling present with the gentle instructions I heard. Then I found myself getting a bit irritated, which quickly turned into feeling *very* irritated. "Who is she to be telling me to do this thing and that thing?" I started to feel like I couldn't stand her — this nice woman who I got along very well with. I was just about to get up from the pillow and quit, when I remembered the instructor telling us that we might encounter a number of upsets in our practice. In those instances, we should do our best to simply be present with whatever we were feeling.

So I did. I kept breathing while I felt a massive irritation towards this woman. As I kept breathing, all of a sudden a flash of insight hit me, and I broke into tears. I saw that I was almost always kind and understanding with the people in my life; usually I cut everyone a good amount of slack if they made a mistake or acted out of selfishness. But there was someone I was leaving out of that loving and gentle perspective. *Me.* I could see how hard I was on myself so much of the time, and that I was as deserving of compassion and caring as everyone around me. As the tears started to fade, I felt an amazing uplift and happiness. This unconscious burden had been released from my being!

As time went on, I knew I wanted to extend this kind of help to others, so I became a massage therapist and began learning about energy healing and meditation. I also saw a psychotherapist for about four years, using talk therapy to help heal my past. Meanwhile I kept learning about more varieties of healing. I studied shiatsu, Bowenwork®, channeling, Quantum-Touch®, and sound healing. I read many books about spirituality and the power of the mind. Studying under energy healer Cindy Libman led me into conscious experiences of some of my past lives.

One day in early 2006, I left my apartment in the suburbs of Chicago, determined to make a difference. I had just received a plea for help from one of my favorite bookstores, and I was going to answer the call. Transitions Bookstore was an institution on the Chicago spiritual scene, holding classes with inspirational teachers and serving as the central hub for many spokes of spiritual thinking that existed in the community. But the bookstore was not in great shape. Their finances were shaky, and they were going to have to close if things didn't get drastically better and fast.

I had opened my mind to a whole world of new ideas in the previous five years. Little did I know, as I got into my car that day, that I was about to usher in a radically different and profound way of thinking and being! I wandered through the store and started putting book after book into my basket. Most from teachers and authors I had heard of before, but one found its way into my basket even though I didn't know who had written it. It was called *A Course in Miracles,* and its principles of non-duality were about to change my life forever. Transitions ended up going out of business a few months later, but their call for help ended up providing me with the answer to the unconscious call for help I had been making my whole life (and in every lifetime before that, as I would learn).

Studying *A Course in Miracles* (also called ACIM or simply, the Course) has revealed to me some big ideas:

God is real.
God is Love.
Nothing else is real, which includes everything in time and space.
I am truly at home in oneness with God, dreaming that I'm a body that's trying to make its way through an unreal temporal world.
My true purpose here is to wake up to that oneness, and know the Love that I am.

I am quite certain that the non-dualistic truths that the Course teaches are so. It makes sense to me, at least intellectually. Only what is eternal, loving, kind, and unchanging is real. All else is not, and that list includes a lot of things. In fact, it includes every *thing* — every concrete, discernible object. Pure love is abstract, beyond form, changeless. This world of time holds only what is bound to change. There is nothing in this world of time that doesn't start, end, or change states, again and again and again. Thus there is nothing in this world that is true.

This is where the terror comes in. Being so identified with a body, as all of us are, the idea that what I am is completely formless feels terrifying, even as a part of me knows that it is true. I find myself oscillating back and forth between accepting this idea with a sense of peace, and pushing it away with the distraction of the moment. It is this concept of identity that is such a fixture in the Course, and one of the underpinnings of what it continuously trains me to do. As I question my identity as a body, in so many subtle and profound ways, I find myself letting go of attachments of how I think the world and my life should look, becoming more peaceful in situations which had previously been upsetting, and knowing a deeper sense of grace is by my side in everything I do.

The ego (that part of mind which believes in separation) keeps telling me that this letting-go of my old, unreal identity is a big deal — and a scam, a dangerous road to travel down. That's because the ego is always convinced that the body is all that I am, and to let go of it will be my complete undoing. What the ego will never tell me is that this undoing is *its* undoing, and that as this happens I am simultaneously stepping into the light, the truth, the reality of Love. This dynamic is why all the shifts I go through on my healing path have a certain amount of upset and fear (from a hint to a high-pitched wail) as they approach, and then a welcome release into joy, happiness and peace, as I step beyond them.

The good news is that I always eventually move through the fear, no matter how much I am avoiding or resisting. In the long run, my true desire for love and for joy moves me through the issue that needs releasing. As this has unfolded over and over, it has become abundantly clear to me that I am only ever healing one issue: the idea that I am somehow disconnected, or separate, from God. All the 'issues' of my life are different covers over that same deeper problem. Every time I find a sense of peace with the 'jerk' on the road who almost hit me, or with various time pressures, or with that politician who rattled my cage, what I am really doing is undoing the completely false idea that I am not one with my Creator.

The Course's View On Past Lives

Reincarnation would not, under any circumstances, be the problem to be dealt with now. If it were responsible for some of the difficulties the individual faces now, his task would still be only to escape from them now. If he is laying the groundwork for a future life, he can still work out his salvation only now.
[Manual for Teachers, Section 24.2]

THE COURSE'S message is consistent: our salvation is found in the present moment. Even when I am looking at an issue from another lifetime, I am experiencing the feelings connected to it now. In this way, ACIM is helping us to see that there is no time. Why? Because only what is eternal is true, and the world is not eternal. *"Time is a belief of the ego, so the lower mind, which is the ego's domain, accepts it without question. The only aspect of time that is eternal is now."* [Chapter 5, Section III.6]

With this foundation, it makes sense to me that the Course sidesteps the issue of past lives. If belief in reincarnation is not necessary to each of us for healing, why make it important? We can simply focus on what is happening in our daily life as the focus for forgiveness. At the same time, if we do believe in past lives, as I most definitely do, that is no obstacle either. All I need to do in each moment is forgive whatever is in front of me. Sometimes that is a present-day issue; sometimes it is a memory from earlier in this lifetime; sometimes it is a memory or feeling that goes back to a lifetime before this one. Or I may be worried about the future, what is seemingly yet to come. But I can choose peace about any of these issues only right now, in this very moment. And so I do, practicing the choice of love in this moment as best as I can with every thought that needs healing.

Even though the Course doesn't take a definite stand on reincarnation, there are several passages which imply that we live more than one lifetime as a mortal being. *"The miracle substitutes for learning that might have taken thousands of years."* [Chapter I, Section II.6] This sentence is clearly talking about learning achieved in more than a single human lifetime. To be told that a single shift of mind can undo so much fear and guilt that it replaces the need to live hundreds of lifetimes is astonishing! At the same time, I know that it's true. Regardless, I know that following this path is my lifetime's work.

As the Course says about itself, it is but *"a special form of the universal course. There are many thousands of other forms, all with the same outcome."* [Manual for Teachers, Section I.4] So, we will all find ourselves back within God in the end. Whatever our path, each of us will reawaken to the truth eventually. We can all delay our awakening to light and love by hiding — that is, choosing fear over peace — but in the long run, we can't miss. I can't not be what I am. That's true for us all. The inner call for love will eventually win out over the painful belief in separation.

Our Past Lives Are a Mixed Bag

*We are ready to look more closely at the ego's thought
system because together we have the lamp that will dispel it,
and since you realize you do not want it, you must be ready.*
[Chapter II, Section V.I]

MANY of the past-life memories and experiences that rise
into my awareness are negative or traumatic, challenging
in some way. As I heal them, the suffering or upset they bring
gives way to joy and a sense of freedom. As I shift into peacefulness, I can feel it sinking deeper within me, as various layers of the
ego clear away. The reason that the problems of these lifetimes are
surfacing is because I am focused on healing all the unconscious
suffering in me. I want to go all the way and wake up to my eternal
loving truth. There's no healing required in a happy experience;
we can just enjoy it, and we should. As the Course says: *"We
dedicate this day to the serenity in which God would have you
be. Keep it in your awareness of yourself and see it everywhere
today, as we celebrate the beginning of your vision and the sight
of the real world, which has come to replace the unforgiven
world you thought was real."* [Lesson 75]

When we let go of the shadow of the ego's thought system, all that remains is the light. As I see my determination to go through these shadows strengthening, my overall experience gets lighter and lighter. Sometimes I envision the ego as a large dark boulder. As I keep practicing forgiveness for all the issues of this lifetime or any other, bits and chunks of the boulder chip loose and fall away. Paradoxically, as the old pains I am healing surface in more challenging forms, I am experiencing more freedom and joy. How is that possible? As I increasingly understand that all of this world is a dream, I comprehend that no dream, major or minor, has the power to take away my peace. It can only do so if I give that power away to it; the choice is always mine.

That's not to say I never have joyful past-life memories. Some of my deepest friendships have seemed to be rooted in forms from other lifetimes. One friend of mine has clearly been my mother, and we had a deeply loving relationship in which I was her daughter. Another friend was a fellow seeker of God in a monastery alongside me.

One powerful memory arose in the middle of a massage. The massage therapist had seen me sharing kindness and compassion in a stressful situation at my workplace, and generously offered me a gift of an hour-long session with him. He was very talented, and I quickly saw that I was in for an excellent bodywork session. As the massage progressed a subtle yet profound feeling began to build within me, like the sun nearing the horizon before breaking into the dawn. It started with a warm feeling of love, even though I seemed to barely know this practitioner.

Why did I love him right away? Then it flashed on me that he was my long-lost brother from another life. We had parted ways as we stepped into adulthood, and I had never heard from him again, nor known what had happened to him. We had always been such good friends growing up, always on each other's side. When he left the farm we grew up on to make his way in the wider world, he said he would come back soon. Soon turned to fall, fall to winter, and winter to more winters after that, but he didn't return. I waited more years than I probably should have before I too went out to make my way in the world. There was an empty space in my heart as I began to forge my own path, filled with questions about him that there seemed to be no answers to. Many years later as my life was coming to a close, I died with all my questions about him unanswered.

And here he was, giving me an amazing massage. Words to describe what I was feeling failed me, but I managed to convey the awareness of our connection somewhat during the massage, and more so afterwards. I could tell by the tears in his eyes that he was deeply moved by my sharing. It was a profound reunion of two souls, releasing the old sense of disconnection that I had unknowingly carried with me through all these many years and lives. As I left his massage studio afterwards, I felt so much lighter — mentally, physically and spiritually.

My Life as a Warrior

The darkest of your hidden cornerstones holds your
belief in guilt from your awareness.
[Chapter 13, Section II.3]

YEARS before that, something in me just didn't feel right. Coming into a workshop with Cindy Libman, my energy healing instructor, I was starting to understand that before a healing, challenging and uncomfortable feelings will sometimes intensify before the healing moves through. I had heard it referred to as 'simmering,' as though a flame was slowly increasing. Something in me was definitely bubbling up.

I did my best to be present in the opening meditation, but kept falling into irritable, upset thoughts, mentally blaming others in my life for not doing what I thought they should. This was definitely not the peaceful, calm feeling I usually got from these meditations.

Cindy's previous workshop in Chicago, my first one with her, had been wonderful. I had gotten in touch with deeply buried issues from my childhood through her combination of psychotherapeutic approaches and deeply insightful energy healing modalities. I remember leaving that event on a cloud. I felt so clear and free from old, unconscious issues within me. This one was shaping up quite differently.

As we moved into the next part of the workshop, we each partnered with another participant. Between us, my partner and I decided that he would receive first, which meant that I would facilitate the energy healing by holding space for him. He lay down on a cushion on the floor, and I sat beside him. As he began to go into his emotions and a deeper experience of his inner state, I held space for him by witnessing his experience free of all judgment, and gently encouraging him on. It felt like the most normal and regular thing to be compassionately present with him in this way.

Then it was my turn to be energetically held and seen by my partner. Cindy and her assistant moved among the pairs of participants, guiding and supporting the participants' facilitation of healing for their partner. I started naming what I was feeling: disgust, guilt, shame, rage. Where were these feelings coming from? I didn't yet know.

The feelings continued to merge and move through, until they seemed to coalesce into just one: terrible, heavy, painful guilt. I had done something terrible; I couldn't escape it. It felt like it was crushing me. But what had I done? And then I knew.

I saw in my mind so clearly that I had swung a sword and killed a man — a soldier I was battling against. This felt similar to the revelation of hidden or suppressed childhood memories, except I knew I hadn't done this in this lifetime. I had never been in battle, nor fought someone with a sword. Thus I realized a past life was coming up to heal. This had never happened to me before and the revelation was astonishing! I had heard others having this type of experience before, but I never knew how much to believe in it. This experience was coming in so strongly and deeply that all doubt of the possibility of past lives was erased from my mind. This was an authentic experience.

The excitement and wonder of actually having a past life experience took me partially out of the exercise's focus of feeling my emotions. Helpfully, my partner encouraged me to go back into what I was feeling, and share it with him. I tuned back into the feeling of horrific guilt, crying heavy, sad tears.

Even though what happened had been part of my role in that life — killing the enemy as a soldier on a battlefield — on a deep soul level, I had absorbed the guilt and pain over the action I had taken. I had been carrying around this horrible guilt and suffering on a deep unconscious level for all this time, through every lifetime I had lived since then.

And now it was coming up, to be seen and healed. Deep, body-shaking sobs came out of me as I felt the awful pain of taking another's life. How could I ever cope with this? I didn't know, but I knew my only job was to allow it all, and that's what I did. I allowed the pain, shame, anger, blame, hatred of myself, and so much more to flow through me, wave after wave of deep and intense emotions.

Eventually, the intensity of the emotions started to subside, like the passing of an intense storm. And then it was done. I knew a lot of the pain and suffering related to this trauma had been released. I had been freed of the heaviness of this memory, and I felt so light! A whole new world of deep, inner exploration had been opened up to me. I didn't know in that moment how promi-nent healing past lives would become in my life.

I would soon learn that most past-life recognitions are subtle and understated. They don't usually surface as mind-blowing recollections or vivid dream experiences. They can be experiences that happen in a normal day — like meeting someone for the first time and having a sense of familiarity, yet not being able to place where you know them from. Or it may be going on vacation to a new place and recognizing that this isn't your first time there — in this lifetime, at least. Or even reading about a different part of the world and feeling a deep sense of comfort or knowledge about that place you've only ever read about or seen on TV. These experiences are common; almost everyone has them.

Past life experiences are still generally dismissed, denied, or minimized in our society. The life-changing results of these kinds of healing experiences speak for their validity, however. Modern-day spiritual teachers are bringing reincarnation more to the forefront of our cultural discussion, bolstered by its deep roots in a number of Eastern spiritual paths. Those who want to explore this topic more deeply now have a wealth of books and articles about past lives to explore. It is a fortuitous time to be discovering our spiritual histories.

Hesitantly Entering the World

*No spark of life but was created with your glad consent,
as you would have it be. And not one Thought that God
has ever had but waited for your blessing to be born.*
[Chapter 30, Section II.I]

THROUGHOUT my life, I've heard the story of my being born into this world. As my mom told it, I didn't seem to be too keen on this place. She went into labor sometime around my due date in mid-October, 1977. She and my dad rushed to the hospital, only to be told by the doctor that her contractions had stopped and she should go back home. Around a week later, the contractions resumed, and again ended when she arrived at the hospital. So they headed back home once more. The third time labor started, about two weeks after my due date, my mom was certain that this was the time. They headed back to the hospital, about an hour's drive from where they lived. And yet again, labor ended when she got to the hospital, except this time my mom was determined. She said, "I am not going home. This baby needs to be born." They induced labor, and the delivery proceeded after that. I hesitantly came into the world on October 29th.

Years later, I was in another healing workshop with Cindy

when this backstory showed itself to me. As I lay there on a mat and gently closed my eyes, the soft rustlings of the other participants settling in to their own spaces began to fade. Cindy's words led me to experience a place of deep, inner restfulness. This state, however, didn't last long, as another feeling came forward that was not nice at all. It was a feeling of pain, suffering, constriction. I felt very small, in a dark and very warm place. All of a sudden, I knew I was in the womb, but not my mother's womb; it was another mother, from an earlier life. I could feel my love for her. She had cared for me so well. But something was wrong — the umbilical cord was strangling me. It was time for me to start coming out, but the pushing only wrapped the cord tighter around my neck. The pain was intense. I wasn't going to make it this time. I blacked out from the pain and the pressure. I didn't wake up in that body again.

As the experience of my painful, stillborn death began to fade, I turned in my mind to the message of the Course: *"God says there is no death; your judgment sees but death as the inevitable end of life."* [Manual for Teachers, Section II.2] I could see that this experience was helping me release the concept of death, as I turned more and more to the certainty of my real life as one with God. An 'Aha!' came to me, about why I hadn't wanted to be born in this lifetime. My earlier dying during childbirth had me terrified as hell about the process. I was going to stay in my mom's womb as long as I could. Thank goodness I didn't have to go through something like that this time.

Is All of This a Hologram?

*This course can therefore be summed up very simply
in this way:* **Nothing real can be threatened.
Nothing unreal exists.** *Herein lies the
peace of God.* [Introduction]

WHEN I was young, I was a huge fan of science fiction and
fantasy books, toys, and games. I had a great time reading and being absorbed into the stories of characters on faraway
planets or traveling through deep space, overcoming obstacles as
they discovered exciting new places. Their adventures became
my adventures. One of the real gems in this category wasn't a
book, but a TV show: *Star Trek: The Next Generation*. The characters on the show were inquisitive and brave, always getting into
situations that required ingenuity and determination in order to
make it through. I always loved it when Captain Picard would say
to his crew, "Make it so."

The creators of the show 'made something so' that was novel
to me at the time, and probably to a lot of other people as well: the
holodeck. This was a virtual reality room on board the starship
that was exceedingly realistic. At times the characters would go
into the holodeck, lose track of what was happening, and not be

able to turn it off and get out of the experience. They were stuck in an experience that wasn't real, but definitely seemed so.

This is what the Course is teaching; that each of us is having an experience that isn't real, even though it seems so. *"This world is not the Will of God, and so it is not real."* [Lesson 166] We have all stepped onto the holodeck of this life that we think is ours, and for the most part, forgotten what we have done. Now we are being asked to wake up. This means to come to realize that what we are experiencing is not reality, and by relinquishing belief in it, to let ourselves come into the experience of true Love, Light, and Joy. This is the experience of our Truth, which has been temporarily obscured by this virtual reality experience of time and space that we seem to be living.

It is clear that we, as a culture, are stepping towards that holodeck type of experience through technology. Virtual reality equipment and worlds are getting more and more elaborate and detailed, and before long we may be having virtual reality experiences as lifelike as the world around us is now. There may be a temptation to use these worlds as a means of escape, to avoid the problems and challenges that we are facing.

There is also a spiritual message behind the virtual reality experience. It comes down to the question: What is real? This physical world of time and space feels real — each of us thinks it's actually happening. The Course pops the bubble of this idea:

"Let not your eyes behold a dream; your ears bear witness to illusion. They were made to look upon a world that is not there; to hear the voices that can make no sound.... For eyes and ears are senses without sense, and what they see

and hear they but report. It is not they that hear and see, but you, who put together every jagged piece, each sense-less scrap and shred of evidence, and make a witness to the world you want. Let not the body's ears and eyes perceive these countless fragments seen within the gap that you imagined, and let them persuade their maker his imaginings are real." [Chapter 28, Section V.5]

This message that the world is not real, and neither are the bodies contained within it, is usually a very jarring one, since it refutes the very core of our mistaken identity: I am an individual self. A part of us, the ego self, doesn't want to consider that we aren't an individual, because a full acceptance of this concept would be the ego's undoing. As long as a part of us is identified as an individual, fully accepting that the world is just a dream will lead to experiences of fear and even outright terror. Facing this fear with as much gentleness and patience as we can find within ourselves is the avenue to its undoing. As we start to come to terms with this idea, this angry terror within gradually gives way to the love and joy that is our natural state of being.

At first, letting go of the belief that we are individuals seems like a loss, like we're losing something important and real. But what's not initially seen is that all we're losing is the idea of separation. As that false mask of the lonely ego slides away, our real Self then shines forward, with nothing obstructing our unconditional joy and love. This truth within us can show us how to live the rest of our lives free from fear, suffering, and pain of any kind. Knowing this world is as unreal as the holodeck allows us to live our lives here with greater kindness. When we are less attached to what is unfolding here, we can think more clearly and see more readily what options within the hologram are in everyone's highest good.

The ego's version of reality is: If the separation from God is true, then this world of separation (the world of time and space) is true. Then we take our experience of this world as proof that the separation is true. But both the separation and this world are actually false. We're trying to use our false experience of this world to show that the false idea supporting it is true, but it's actually just one layer of false beliefs after another. None of it's real. To the ego, seeing this idea is terrifying, although it actually holds the key to undoing our inner experience of imprisonment. The more we begin to accept this idea, the more peace will show up in our lives.

"If you could recognize that <u>your only problem is separation,</u> no matter what form it takes, you could accept the answer because you would see its relevance. Perceiving the underlying constancy in all the problems that seem to confront you, you would understand that you have the means to solve them all." [Lesson 79; emphasis mine]

A New Understanding of Miracles

*Because reality is changeless is a miracle already there
to heal all things that change, and offer them to you to see
in happy form, devoid of fear. It will be given you to look
upon your brother thus.* [Chapter 30, Section VIII.5]

THE COURSE has taught me that healing is all about how I look at things. The specifics of the situation are never crucial; what matters is how I am looking at what's occurring. In the beginning, I tended to be more preoccupied with circumstances. Over time, I have found it easier to focus on my perceptions. Now, worldly conditions are less likely to throw me off balance. Why? Because I am more diligent in remembering my power to see things differently, rather than giving them power over me. The result is a greater sense of well-being.

To help us make this inward transition, ACIM uses Christian and Western terminology, yet often gives new and more helpful meanings to these words. The word 'miracle' is a primary example. We all know what a miracle is, right? When something that seems physically impossible occurs after a whole lot of praying, that's a miracle. That's how the word miracle is typically understood, anyway. In the Course, the miracle is defined as an inner shift of perception. *"As an expression of what you truly are, the miracle places the mind in a state of grace."* [Chapter I, Section III.7] *"The holy light you saw outside yourself, in every miracle you offered to your brothers, will be returned to you."* [Chapter 13, Section VIII.8]

In *A Course in Miracles*, miracles are the same as forgiveness, representing a shift within the mind away from judgment, fear or division, toward love, oneness and joy. This is the "change of mind" we have to pursue repeatedly.

The more we pay attention to our inner state of being, the more we will see how we fall into ego thought patterns in every kind of situation. I can see it in myself. Someone in my life says or does the 'wrong' thing, and my inner judgment machine is off and running:

"They wouldn't say that if they really loved me."

"They're not so enlightened."

"*I* would never do that!"

And on and on…

What is the miracle? It means catching myself when I've jumped back on the ego hamster wheel of repetitive judgments, then remembering I don't really want to do that. I don't really want to blame. I don't really want to choose a destructive thought system that always ends up with me holding the unhappy bag of misery.

And why is that always the result? It's actually because *there is only one of us.* That means whenever I'm blaming, hating, or judging someone else, that energy is going to come back to me. It truly has nowhere else to go. So the miracle happens when I choose to let all of that go. I can feel the relief and freedom that comes from handing over the old, tired thought system I've been clinging to since my very first lifetime. Our awakening to oneness with Love is called "atonement" in the Course, another reinterpretation of a traditional Christian term. It is a collection of all these inner choices for peace instead of anger and upset. *"Miracles are part of an interlocking chain of forgiveness which, when completed, is the Atonement."* [Chapter I, Section I.25]

A Glimpse Backward

Only love is strong because it is undivided. The strong
do not attack because they see no need to do so.
[Chapter 12, Section V.I]

PAIN... A fog of fear, uncertainty... Emotions merging into an awful, tremendous guilt. This cloud of emotions coalesced into a memory: I had pressed the button. I was flying with my squadron over enemy territory, thinking "They deserve what they're getting." Hard-jawed and with a steely focus, I was the bombardier, dropping massive destruction onto the chosen targets, killing the 'bad guys' and anyone else who happened to get in the way. People I cared about, fellow soldiers who were my friends, had fallen to their last attack, and I was sure as hell going to give them my best in return. I didn't choose the places that we dropped the bombs, but I gladly fulfilled my function.

Back in this life, I was aching with the pain of the death and destruction. Every time we commit an act of violence, no matter how 'justified' or 'popular,' our soul is burdened until we are ready to forgive and release it. Breathing, I simply allowed the emotions to surface — pain, shame, guilt, rage — a maelstrom of feelings coursing through me. In the original experience, I couldn't afford to experience all this, and wasn't conscious of most of it anyhow. I just bottled it up, and now here it was, spilling up and out, a sense of pain shifting into a gradual relief.

My breath continued. The memory and pain and shame settled back down. I felt a sense of relief and healing, as though a heavy cloak I had been carrying around all unknown had just been lifted from my shoulders.

Cindy encouraged us to come back from the group healing meditation. The emotions and memory receded further, as I began to find myself in my surroundings. The other nine participants in the class were coming to as well, stretching as they continued to release the remnants of their old feelings.

As we gathered into a circle, we were invited to share any of our experiences that we felt called to. I volunteered my past life story of bombing and killing, regret and shame, as well as the beautiful gift of grace as I was unburdened, like a dark shadow melting before dawn's gentle rays. As I shared, I was greeted by several knowing smiles, kind and unjudging, knowing that a profound healing was taking place within me. Others shared as well, childhood pains and traumas mixing with sometimes obscure and abstract issues. Kindness and a release of pain were common elements in all our stories.

Participating in Cindy Libman's energy healing classes had been eye-opening and deeply healing for me. I had gotten in touch with so much that I had either suppressed or simply didn't know was within. The open-hearted experiences I was having were deeply liberating and an indication that I was making headway on my path. Others' experiences only served to reinforce the new perspectives I was realizing were true. I was seeing that all my issues in life could shift toward healing if I allowed that loving influence within to come forward and unfold. Acts of unkindness, including actual violence, were capable of being healed by gently witnessing them with care and kindness.

At the heart of the Course's teachings is the idea that there is only one problem, and that is the belief that we are separate from God. We are not really separate, but it's certainly true that we *believe* it, usually at a deep and unconscious level. This belief is so existentially painful and horrific that we have collectively pushed it out of our minds. This pushing, which you could also call projection, is still happening, and is painful and destructive for all of us. By pushing away the guilt and suffering caused by believing that we have done the unthinkable, we maintain the material world of separation that we see.

Our whole experience of time and space is a testament to the idea that separation is real. Time seems to be divided into past, present and future. Then the past and the future can be further sub-divided — an hour ago, a day ago, a year ago, a millennium ago. What is here now was not here then, and will not be here in the future. Time seems to prove that change is real, but it is not. It is simply an experiential delusion.

Space also seems to prove that separation is the truth. My body occupies a different place in space than your body; the window I am looking out while I write this is separate from me in space. The tree in the backyard is separate. All things and bodies seem to prove the separation real. What we don't usually recognize is that this whole universe was made up *to prove the separation is true*. The idea of separation came first in the mind, and the world is nothing but an unreal effect.

Practicing the Workbook

[I]t is doing the exercises that will make the goal of the
course possible. An untrained mind can accomplish nothing.
[Workbook Introduction]

THE COURSE is ultimately a way of life. Adopting this
spiritual mindset again and again and again is an ongoing
practice, as we wind our way through the tumultuous journey
that each of us experiences in embodiment. For anyone who feels
called to make it their path, the ideas that it shares reinforce our
essence as resistance to its loving message gradually falls away.
Eventually the love is all that is left. That is our truth. That is our
joy. That is our peace.

That day back in 2006 when I picked up my first copy of
ACIM, I had no clue about any of this. I had a spiritual practice
and a number of different teachings I was doing my best to apply.
Yet I had never encountered a non-dualistic spiritual path before.
When I got back home with the Course, I attempted to read it.
It didn't go so well; a pattern emerged where I would read a few
pages and fall asleep. A day or so later, I would read another page
or three, and zonk out again. After a handful of attempts, I had

gotten no farther than page 13 in the Text.

I was surprised but not entirely deterred. I decided to change tactics and focus on the Workbook. For those of you new to the Course, it is comprised of three main sections and some additional material. First, there is the 600-plus page Text, which has the bulk of ACIM's teachings and theoretical framework. Next there is a Workbook, with 365 daily lessons. After that comes the Manual for Teachers and some additional sections which further elucidate the teaching.

I got the feeling that the short lessons that begin the Workbook wouldn't be too much for me to do. I was even encouraged by the Introduction not to worry if I didn't understand the ideas shared in the Workbook. All I had to do was the best I could, and the benefits would come from the practice. With that bit of wind to uplift my studies, I started with Workbook Lesson 1: *"Nothing I see in this room [on this street, from this window, in this place] means anything."*

The Course is not messing around! It starts right away with some power-packed concepts.

I did my best with practicing the Workbook. Sometimes I would skip a day or two, but I would just keep right on going and get back into it. I didn't always get what it was saying, but I tried not to worry about that. Many times, I would forget the daily lesson or practice almost immediately after reading it, and perhaps rarely think about it until the end of the day when I saw it by my bedside once again. Sometimes I even actively resisted and avoided the practices. As counseled by the Workbook itself, I did what I could to release any self-judgment around my seeming lack of diligence.

After about nine months of doing the Workbook, I found another book that totally broke open my confusion and gave me so much clarity about the Course's message. Sitting on a table display at Barnes & Noble was a book entitled *The Disappearance of the Universe* by Gary Renard. The cover interested me, and when I checked in with my intuition to see if I should get it, the answer was clear: "Why not?"

This book cleared some Course cobwebs for me. With humor and plain-spoken language, the key concept of forgiveness was clearly explained. I also learned such foundational ideas as nonduality, the stages of the spiritual path, and why the Course is almost always a long spiritual path for the people who practice it. We're extremely resistant to awakening, and unconsciously terrified of genuinely embracing and practicing the concepts of ACIM. I knew I would keep on going through the resistance I was feeling, and increasingly come to experience the release from fear that is the Course's promise to all of us.

"Your sinlessness is guaranteed by God. Nothing can touch it, or change what God created as eternal." [Lesson 93]

Layers of the Onion

*And so each instant given unto God in passing, with the
next one given Him already, is a time of your release from
sadness, pain and even death itself.* [Lesson 194]

I HAVE been told that healing our unconscious guilt over the
seeming separation from God is like peeling back the layers of
an onion. After peeling a layer or two of the onion back, you're
still left with an onion — a smaller onion, but it can still make you
cry. Well, I can definitely see how this plays out in my life.

One of my issues in this life is my relationship with food.
Since I was a kid, I've fluctuated between being skinny and heavy.
I often look at food as a source of comfort, or even a way to soften
the blows that this world often lands on us. It isn't unusual for me
to look for some happiness in the bottom of a dish of ice cream or a
bag of chips, even if I know it isn't really there. Studying *A Course
in Miracles* has helped to change this for me, although the change
is definitely in the slow-and-steady category.

One of the first changes I noticed was a new capacity for
recognizing I had choices. This might come to awareness as I was
about to reach for the food out of a sense of need, or after I had
been unconsciously eating for a while. Whenever the awareness

surfaced, I would make one of two decisions: either I would keep eating, or I would stop. Yet in either case, I felt less guilt! Even if I ate a whole box of cookies, I wouldn't feel so upset with myself at the end. This was a subtle yet significant shift in the way I was addressing this issue.

Another thing I noticed is that my need to eat from a sense of lack began to ease. As I was healing this false but seemingly real hole in my spiritual sense of being, this need to keep throwing food down the hatch to try to fill a bottomless void also began to release. Now there are times in my life when I can have a box of sweets in the kitchen and not feel compelled to eat them all. Not that I don't get a serious case of the munchies now and again, but it's all about making headway.

As I keep healing, I am understanding more and more that the body is not what I am. What I really am is Spirit, which is synonymous with Truth and Love. This truest expression of my identity is beyond form, time, and space. This is hard to articulate because it is beyond all concepts, and thus not possible for the separated mind to grasp. What is possible is to recognize pointers, or arrows, that lead to this experience, and that's what all the discussions about God or Spirit in the Course help to do.

So I often come to see that this formless, unending Love is what I am, but sometimes I then flip over to being terrified of it — and food is often the way I try to cover the fear. Fear almost always feels intense, way more than I can handle in the moment. But if I don't numb myself out by eating, watching TV, or another distraction, I can move through the emotion and eventually emerge on the other side. From this new point of view, I'm often amazed at how insignificant the previously intense terror has become.

I see that it wasn't at all like I had thought it was, as the energy and upset was building. I try to remember this perspective as new challenges come my way, realizing that they aren't what they seem to be, which helps to disarm the upset before it gets out of hand.

Oftentimes, the hardest part about all of this is remembering that there is a different perspective I can choose about the challenge. When I'm in the thick of it, I find myself rushing to judge and condemn, to find someone, anyone, to take the blame, as long as it doesn't rest on me. But more and more, I am seeing that the path to Truth lies in taking responsibility for whatever is coming my way. *"I am not a victim of the world I see"* [Lesson 31] — I am the director and screenplay writer. And I can decide not to be afraid of the movie I made, especially since it's not even real. It's all just a dream. Thank God! And pass the popcorn. (But not the whole bowl!)

Overtones, Harmonics, Echoes

The real sound is always a song of thanksgiving and of Love.
You cannot, then, ask for the echo. It is the song that is the gift.
Along with it come the overtones, the harmonics, the echoes,
but these are secondary. In true prayer you hear only the song.
All the rest is merely added. [Song of Prayer, Section I.I]

A S I KEEP working on forgiving my upsets and problems, I develop a better understanding of this quote. I always want my goal to be peace, and this can be true no matter what I am doing. My world doesn't need to look a certain way in order for me to choose open-heartedness and compassion. This has been my ongoing practice, and even though I'm not always good at it in the moment, I'm getting better. The sooner I choose love, the less I suffer.

As we keep choosing love, the sweet harmonics begin to show up as well — that is, mystical experiences deepen and become more constant. The sense of God being with me is stronger all the time, helping me to know that I am never alone.

One of these "harmonics" showed up when I was heading to Erie, Pennsylvania, with my friend E. Jason Gremley, for a retreat centered around love, freedom and the teachings of *A Course in*

Miracles. We had a lot of laughter on the drive from Chicago. In addition to being a great friend, Jason has always taught me not to take things too seriously. Nothing ever stays heavy for too long when we're together. The weekend was a real joy and blessing; I shared a workshop on healing past-life karma, and it was well-received even if some of the attendees weren't too keen on the whole past-life idea.

The property was part of a peaceful monastery situated on Lake Erie, but there was no lake access available. A bunch of us, including Jason and me, found a gap in the fence and decided it was time to go swimming. Some people waded in with their shoes on since this part of the shore was quite rocky; Jason and I decided to go for it barefoot and jumped into the cool and refreshing water. After swimming a short distance, we both stood up only to discover the rocks beneath our feet were covered in sharp mollusks or mussels. It was clear from each other's expressions that we had both been hurt; the sharp shell edges had definitely pierced through the skin on one of my feet. The same had happened to Jason.

Rather than react with fear or upset, we both decided to go within. After finding a place in the water away from the sharp-edged shells, we went into meditation together. I allowed the pain to be in my awareness as I moved through a forgiveness process: I reminded myself that the pain wasn't really coming from my body, but from my mind. If I went to the core of the pain, I would see that it was rooted in my belief that I had separated from God. But in truth there is no separation from God, hence there could be no pain, mental or otherwise. The real truth in me was only immortal spirit, which could not be lost regardless of what seemed to happen in an unreal world.

    I let these thoughts wash through my mind as I kept releasing the pain and joining with the Light within. After a few minutes, I was surprised to find that my foot didn't hurt at all. When Jason opened his eyes, he was smiling as well. We swam a little more and then headed ashore. When I looked at my foot, I could see that the cuts had mostly healed in just that short time, and were not bleeding although they had been deep enough to do so. The cuts continued to heal over the next day or two without the need for bandages or extra care. This happy "overtone" helped me to see that my peace of mind really didn't depend on the things of the world "going my way" or fitting my ideas of what should unfold. What a blessing!

Exercise

Know Thyself

*Bring this light fearlessly with you, and bravely hold it up
to the foundation of the ego's thought system. Be willing to
judge it with perfect honesty. Open the dark cornerstone of
terror on which it rests, and bring it out into the light. There
you will see that it rested on meaninglessness, and that
everything of which you have been afraid was based
on nothing.* [Chapter II, Introduction]

THIS IS an opportunity to bring forward for healing the dark
and upset issues within yourself.

Take out a piece of paper and write the first category on it that
pops out at you from this list:

Job/Career

Romantic Relationship

Health

Friends

Money

Family

Childhood

Religion/Spirituality

Below this category on your paper, write down a short description of one to three issues or challenges that you find upsetting in this part of your life.

One at a time, focus in on these issues within yourself. Let your eyes close, and call on the Light within to be with you. Then simply bear witness to this challenging situation with the Light by your side. Breathe with it for up to a few minutes, then gently hand the whole issue over to the Light and let go the best you can.

Being an Outcast

If you did not feel guilty you could not attack, for condemnation is the root of attack. It is the judgment of one mind by another as unworthy of love and deserving of punishment.
[Chapter 13, Introduction]

I COULD feel tension in my shoulders, neck and throat. *Stay with it,* said my inner guidance. I took a deep breath and allowed this uncomfortable sensation to just be. I wanted to get away, and I had made that choice before, many times: the choice to start eating, or read aimlessly, watch TV, surf online. But not this time. This time I listened as the sensations intensified. A portal within opened, and I knew that a new past life was surfacing.

Bits and pieces of emotions and memories flew into my awareness: shame, sadness, pain. And a feeling of being judged: *Why wouldn't anyone stand up for me?*

I had been caught making a poultice, a treatment for an ailment, using techniques and methods that weren't approved of by my culture.

"How did you know to use that herb?" they asked me.

"I don't know. I just do."

"A tool of Satan. Witch. She has the curse," rumbled the

crowd. "How did you know to make it like that? No one we know does it that way."

"I just know. The heart knows." There was no doubt in my mind that the poultice would help my friend's ailment.

But the crowd grew louder. "She is a tool of the devil. Cast her out! She has no place here. She will bring more misfortunes on us, like the little boy who got ill and died. What did you have to do with his death? And what do you know of this drought?"

"What? That was a tragedy. I didn't have anything to do with that, with any of that."

But the crowd had made up its mind. I was the bad one, I was their scapegoat. I didn't even have time to go home and gather my few belongings before I was run out of town. The emotions from this whole experience coursed through me now: shame, abandonment, the conviction that life was cruel and unfair. While I was feeling all this, I did my best to cling less tightly. The emotions began to subside, and I began to feel a new healing surface. No wonder I'd been feeling uncertain about sharing the gifts and spiritual messages that had been coming into my awareness recently. Knowing what had happened to me in another life as a young woman, it made sense that I would clam up rather than talk with people about my experiences now.

However, I knew on a soul level that nothing as drastic as banishment would happen now. I could share without fear of being punished. What a relief! This opening helped free me to step more into the public eye. The reluctance I had been feeling about leading classes on spirituality, and even writing my books to share with the world, was melting away.

Turning the Corner

The opposite of joy is depression. When your learning
promotes depression instead of joy, you cannot be listening
to God's joyous Teacher and learning His lessons.
[Chapter 8, Section VII.13]

E VERYONE on a spiritual path has gone through rough times
and thought, "What is this path doing for me? Is it even
working?" Such doubts seem to be universal. Spiritual principles
and practices seem to benefit us for a while; we feel more peaceful
or happy or just less upset than previously. Then the ego takes
us over again and we feel like we're back where we started, or
even worse.

I've had such ups and downs on my journey while clearing
the karma of past lives, as well as handling the guilt connected
to this life. This issue showed up as a feeling of general "stuck-
ness" and low motivation. In these funks, I would not want to do
the very things I knew made me happy. You could call it a minor
depression; the official diagnosis was low-level bipolar disorder.

As I began the Course I found myself being cautiously
hopeful that this spiritual path could help me with this pervasive
pattern. And it did, if only in fits and starts for a while. When I

found myself in another round of the unpleasantly familiar stuck-ness, I used the forgiveness steps on the experience, layer after layer after layer. I realized I wasn't really upset because I was failing to take action on promoting my business, or I wasn't reaching out to a retreat center where I wanted to lead a workshop, and so on. My lack of action was not the real cause of my upset. The upset was already in me (around the thought of separation from God), and I was projecting that deep metaphysical pain onto the situation of feeling stuck.

But the separation never happened, and the physical world that resulted hadn't really happened either. On the level of true oneness, *nothing happened*, not even my experience of avoiding progress on my worldly purpose. Nothing had ever actually happened that I could feel guilty about. Nothing at all. So I'd reach out to the Holy Spirit in my mind and ask for help to see the real innocence in me and in everything about this situation.

Most of the time, this made me feel at least a bit better, sometimes a lot. Sometimes when I was feeling better, I would take action on whatever I felt blocked from doing. For instance, as I was just beginning my path as an energy healer, I had the idea to put on a workshop about choosing love and light more often in our daily lives. The ego kept blocking me with fear and inaction, however. After a few weeks of not doing anything except handing over my fear to Spirit, I decided to go for a walk. As I left my apartment, I got a nudge to walk a different direction than I generally did. After a block I noticed that I was walking in the direction of my church — the very place I was wanting to put on this workshop! I was being nudged by Spirit to walk right into the church office and find out how to organize an event. As it turns out, they were receptive to the idea, and I ended up leading my first spiritual workshop there.

This feeling of flow has gradually increased in my life, as the ego's anxiety has waned. As the years have passed, feeling unmotivated or stuck has been mostly released. I still have my moments of resistance and fear, but they are not as intense or long-lasting as they were before I started ACIM's forgiveness practice. I am so deeply grateful for this amazing shift in my life!

The End of Suffering

Suffering is but illusion. [Lesson 155]

O NE OF the messages of *A Course in Miracles* is that suffering is not real. Going through this world often feels sad, but that's because we don't see the unreality of sadness while we are wrapped in the ego's heavy blankets. We also don't see that it's in our power to stand up, shake free from these blankets, and choose love instead. Letting go of being the victim is anathema to the part of us that believes in separation. This part of us, the ego part, which *is* the belief in separation, needs an individual identity to reinforce the idea that we are separate.

What are the strongest declarations of individuality? *I am suffering. I am aggrieved. I am hurt. I am on my own.* All these ideas reinforce me-as-individual. These are the ego's bread and butter; it needs suffering to survive.

The good news for us is that we don't have to choose what the ego wants. We can relinquish our unconscious grip on being an individual, being special, and having things go our way. To most of us, this sounds terrifying: "I don't want to let go of those things!" But as the Course famously asks, ***"Do you prefer that you be right or happy?"*** [Chapter 29, Section VII.2] We may think we want to be happy, but often we act like we want to be right. This dynamic is the reason that the Course is a lifelong spiritual path. We have so much resistance that we fight against it all the way. Consciously, we can say to ourselves: *I want the peace of God, I want the peace of God, I want the peace of God.* But what does the Course say about this in the Workbook lesson with that title?

"I want the peace of God. To say these words is nothing. But to mean these words is everything." [Lesson 185] So all of us might say these words, but almost no one fully means them. If we fully wanted this peace, we would have it all the time, without exception. It is only our fearful resistance to love that keeps it from being our constant experience. God's love is never absent, but it can seem to be as long as we are holding it at bay.

So, how do we stop holding it at bay? This is where the forgiveness process of the Course comes in. It is fairly simple, but it takes practice and persistence to achieve the goal of peace and happiness that is its reward. The first step is remembering that we are never upset for the reason we think [Lesson 5]. It looks like we are upset because that guy bumped into us carelessly, or that person didn't say the words we wanted to hear, or for a myriad of reasons. However, the cause of our upset is *never* something that seems to happen in the world of time and space. The cause of upset is always something within the mind, specifically the belief that we are separate from God. This may show up in many forms, but the belief in separation is always at the root of suffering. The first step of healing is thus **Reversing Projection**, which requires recognizing that we have taken our inner suffering and tried to push it out onto a painful scenario that is playing out in our lives, whatever that may be.

The next step is to realize that not only is suffering not coming from "out there," it's also not coming from within, because suffering never happened and is not real. Since the separation from God never happened, everything that has seemed to arise from it — the whole world of time and space — never happened either. This step could be called: **Remembering the World is a Dream, And I'm Still One with God.** This is why we are really forgiving what has *not* happened: *"Forgiveness recognizes what you thought your brother did to you has not occurred."* [Workbook, Part II.I] We could also say that forgiveness means releasing our belief that the cause of our upset is real.

The final step is realizing that we cannot do this on our own. We **Call on the Holy Spirit**, or any other symbol of light, to ask for its help in seeing any predicament through eyes of love. We may also want to choose the Holy Spirit's strength of love and peace. Remembering to choose this real strength leads us eventually to psychological invulnerability — the state where nothing this world can throw at us can hurt us. I'm looking forward to that!

As we steadily practice these concepts, we may find them beginning to blend and combine. The experience of forgiving outlined here will become faster, smoother, and easier, whenever we remember to do it. For most of us, that is the hardest part, remembering that the choice to forgive is always available, even when the world seems to be getting in our face. That's why the Course says right away, *"Miracles are habits..."* [Chapter I, Section I.5] If we keep practicing these ideas, they come to mind more easily when they are really needed, whenever things aren't going well. As many people have said about this path: it's simple, but not always easy.

A Terrible Remembering

Whom you perceive as guilty you would crucify.
Yet you restore guiltlessness to whomever you see as guiltless.
Crucifixion is always the ego's aim. It sees everyone as guilty,
and by its condemnation it would kill. The Holy Spirit sees only
guiltlessness, and in His gentleness He would release from fear
and re-establish the reign of love. [Chapter 14, Section V.10]

A S USUAL, my emotions were the entry point into the depth of a past life. Shame, sadness, grief, mourning — this one felt big. I just kept breathing and being with it. I had done something bad — unbelievably bad.

In my mind's eye, there I was with a hammer in one hand and a spike in the other, getting ready to nail a person to the cross they were tied to.

I had heard the rumors and the disbelieving dismissals:

"He was a healer, yeah right."

"Someone said he even brought somebody back from the dead."

"Only an imbecile would believe that!" said another, as they all laughed derisively.

To me, he was just another task for that day at work. The

job was rough and sometimes soul-crushing, but I had been homeless before and never wanted to beg for money again. The Roman Empire was steady and reliable in its pay.

I raised my hammer and swung down hard. It had to be a solid blow for this kind of work. Surprisingly, there was no scream of pain. But he hadn't been unconscious just a second ago.

Turning to look at him, I saw not unconsciousness, but instead a look of pure love, endless compassion, deep kindness. His gaze was gentle and soft, without a hint of anger or recrimination. There was no sign that he was upset or in pain of any kind. His love was awesome and seemed so out of place I had no idea what to make of it. A part of me felt blessed by this completely unguarded expression, yet at the same time I was stunned by its incongruity with the setting. How was it possible that this man, Y'shua, could be so unfazed by being nailed to the cross? It made no sense. What did it mean?

Confused and stunned, I tried to get the others' attention. "Do you see what's happening? He's not like the others. I nailed his wrist, and nothing happened! No shout, no scream, no anything." I couldn't believe it.

One of the other guards said, "Here, let me do it." He took the hammer from me and nailed Y'shua's other wrist to the cross. The steady, loving gaze continued. The guard nailed his feet to the cross, driving the spike harder and deeper than usual. Y'shua's expression was unchanged. The guard then took a spear and drove it into Y'shua's side. Y'shua returned nothing but love. The guard stomped off in anger and frustration.

I was shaken but didn't know what to do. None of the other guards seemed as affected by what we just witnessed as I was.

How could they not be? Why weren't they amazed by this man whose love and peace was untouched by nailed spike or piercing blade? They started to move on to the next prisoner to be put up on a cross, but I stayed a little longer, hardly believing what my eyes were showing me. This man, with compassion and peace in his gaze, was he what they were saying he was? Was he a savior?

"C'mon! Hurry up back there!" one of the guards called. I slowly turned from this stunning scene, moving on to my next tasks with a head full of questions and no apparent answers. My day went on with a swirling sense of confused wonder.

As the memory started to recede, some of the most intense emotions I had ever felt arose within me — emotional wounding, sorrow, wave after wave of relentless guilt. I knew without a shadow of a doubt that I had helped kill Jesus, nailing him to a cross and leaving him to die. A massive sadness flooded through me as I cried heavy, sad tears. In the middle of this pain and suffering, I asked for help. And there he was, Jesus, immediately within my mind, saying: "Nothing happened."

I started to remember what all of this experience was for: forgiveness. Forgiveness, according to the Course, means recalling our projections of guilt, then coming to see that all guilt is unreal, based on nothing but a lie of separation. As I felt the pain, I started to see what Jesus was saying to me was true. The crucifixion hadn't really happened, because *nothing in the world* ever really happened. The pain and guilt I was feeling were therefore baseless, unfounded, unjustified.

The pain and sorrow lessened as I let these ideas flow through me. I still couldn't believe what I had just experienced. Who would believe such a thing? I knew I would keep this experience close to the vest, and in fact many years passed before I shared this memory with more than just a few people.

Letting the Guilt Go

There is no death because the Son of God is like his Father.
Nothing you can do can change Eternal Love. Forget your
dreams of sin and guilt... [Clarification of Terms, Section 5.6]

One of the clearest teachings from *A Course in Miracles* is that my purpose is to allow the guilt in my mind to be undone. I do this through turning to the Holy Spirit any time I have a grievance, judgment, or upset of any kind, and asking for his help. I also ask for help to see my experience through eyes of love instead of hate, anger, or separation of any kind. This is the practice. No matter what I appear to be doing in this world, my deepest reason for being here is to heal the mind of guilt. That guilt can always be traced back to the belief in the separation from God.

Guilt may be the root, but this tree of separation has many branches. Any lack of peace, no matter how mild or severe, is some manifestation of guilt in our awareness. We may call it by many names: fear, sin, shame, sorrow, pain, suffering, bitterness, jealousy, rage, upset, irritation, hatred, uneasiness, feeling disturbed, spooked, shaken, out of sorts, sick, sensitive, and many more. Whenever we are not completely calm and at peace, we can be sure that we are pushing love away in some way. Why? To hold on to our individuality, which is the ego's seeming shield against what it fears as 'oblivion': the eternal reality of oneness and love.

This often brings up the question, "What would I be without my body?" For me, this thought comes with fear bordering on terror. I understand intellectually that what I really am is Spirit, Love, Truth, Oneness — all those good capitalized words in the Course which serve as symbols pointing to God. But on a "gut level," this idea often induces a feeling of complete loss. Because the ego tells me that without my body, I am nothing. And there is a part of me that still believes it.

Sometimes I have this push-pull, tug-of-war feeling as I accept Oneness and then retreat. We are all so deeply rooted in our individuality that to challenge it feels like we are threatening the very basis of what we are. The right-minded part of us, which we call the Holy Spirit, knows that we are only challenging a false idea and that nothing true can actually be threatened. That doesn't stop the ego within us from throwing up all kinds of fears and anxieties about the process of letting all our false layers be undone.

The ego, however, has a fatal flaw: it is not actually real. As we come to accept that, the ego's attempts to scare us become more and more like a toddler's temper tantrum for attention — less and less upsetting to us as we go forward. We can still deal with the situation appropriately, but we don't have to buy into the energy of upset that is behind it.

Ordinary Karma

*[W]hat was once a dream of judgment now has changed into
a dream where all is joy, because that is the purpose that it has.
Only forgiving dreams can enter here, for time is almost over.
And the forms that enter in the dream are now perceived as
brothers, not in judgment, but in love.*
[Chapter 29, Section IX.7]

RECENTLY I was trying to get help for some software I'd installed. Like a lot of American companies, this software company had outsourced their technical support service, so when I called for help I found myself speaking to a gentleman from India. The call started off cordially enough. However, as I described what I was trying to do, it became clear that this gentleman was unable or unwilling to help me. Now, I'm not generally a hot-under-the-collar kind of guy, quite the opposite. Yet, in this situation, I found myself speaking more and more aggressively with him. I was expressing my anger at his inability to resolve my issue and letting him know that I was not happy. After several fruitless rounds of discussion, I ended the call in a fit of anger, bitterness, and righteous indignation.

As I sat there at my desk, I wondered what was happening

in me. I wasn't normally like this. What had caused me to lose my cool and take it out on this man that I had seemingly no connection with? Since I had the time, I closed my eyes and turned within to see where this would take me. The first thing I felt was anger coursing through me; I felt justified because he was in the wrong, and *they* were in the wrong. As I sat with my discomfort, I asked myself, who were 'they'?

And then I felt it: people from India. I could tell I was going into a past life as a rush of images and feelings came to me. They had treated me so wrongly! As an outsider, I had traveled to India because I was unable to find food in the village I had grown up in. Yet, rather than finding a handout or help, I only found derision. Homeless, living on the streets, and not from their town, I felt their unkindness like a knife blade to my spirit. I was devastated and impoverished, and eventually headed back to my homeland, hoping for anything better than this. But the way I'd been treated stayed with me.

As I came back to my current surroundings, I knew this answered some of my questions. It definitely explained my enmity toward the man I'd just been talking with; what actually happened on the call was mostly irrelevant. There was a deep, unconscious, racist thought within me rooted in the painful lifetime I'd glimpsed. The intensity of the ancient trauma was letting go as it was brought to the light within me.

As I thought about it, I wondered why I didn't have this reaction to the friends and classmates of mine at Northwestern who were of Indian descent. Finally I realized that now was just the time. Time for me to see this issue, and time for me to let it heal. Issues can lay dormant within us for decades, even lifetimes, before the time is right for them to surface and be seen. When they shift and release, old unconscious patterns no longer affect us. As this issue healed in me, other subtle and mostly unseen issues around racism were surfacing, which would lead me to have even less unconscious bias in the future. It definitely wasn't fun to go through that experience, but I was feeling more and more grateful that Spirit was guiding me and supporting me in healing all of these upsets in my life.

Spiritual Resentment

Truth has rushed to meet you since you called upon it. If you knew Who walks beside you on the way that you have chosen, fear would be impossible. You do not know because the journey into darkness has been long and cruel, and you have gone deep into it. A little flicker of your eyelids, closed so long, has not yet been sufficient to give you confidence in yourself, so long despised. You go toward love still hating it, and terribly afraid of its judgment upon you. And you do not realize that you are not afraid of love, but only of what you have made of it. [Chapter 18, Section III.3]

DO YOU hate God? Most of us would answer "no." If I am being honest with myself, I have to admit that sometimes the answer is *hell yes!* As I follow my spiritual path I sometimes think that this world has dealt me a bad set of cards (in this lifetime or another) and I feel 'justifiably' aggrieved and generally angry at God for putting me in these circumstances. *A Course in Miracles* teaches the opposite: that God has nothing at all to do with what happens in this world of ups and downs, and in fact is completely beyond this world of dreams. My purpose is actually to wake up to the perfect state of love and joy that is our shared deepest truth.

Most days, though, I don't keep this in the forefront of my mind. When things hit the fan, I just get mad that the world isn't going my way. Believing that something is wrong inevitably leads to needing someone to blame. And God is the perfect scapegoat. Or at least the image of God that we've made up in our minds is to blame. Then the pain of the wrongness doesn't rest on me. This is how the dynamic of projection works: We try to reduce pain within by putting it out onto someone else. What generally goes unseen is that this technique in reality keeps the suffering in place and keeps it from being healed. As I keep continuing to learn how all this works, I am wising up to the myriad ways I use projection to create a false sense of safety.

On the level of the world, it looks like I'm blaming the driver on the road who cuts me off, or someone in my life who says the wrong thing or just doesn't say the right thing. It's their fault, not mine. But on a subtler level, my relationship to God, the same dynamic is playing out. Then I am off the hook for my state of mind. I'm the righteous victim of God! Or at least that's what the ego tells me. But I don't have to keep buying into this way of seeing. The following experience brought this realization home for me.

It could see me. I was scared. I didn't like this anymore. The fear in me bubbled up and I trembled. The pattern had played out enough times that I knew what to do: *Stay with it. Breathe. See where it leads.* As one of my teachers said, "What is the gift in the fear, the pain, the sadness? Be willing to let the treasure reveal itself. It is always there if we go through the storm."

So I stayed with it. But it continued to stare at me dispassionately. What was it exactly, this eye, unblinking and all-seeing?

It was clear that it represented God to me. I was feeling this massive fear of God. A part of me — the conscious part — wanted to know my true Self and to come into the reality of the Love of God. Yet here was this fearful thought: "Why would I want to know a God who allows my friends to die? Why would I want to have anything to do with that?"

I knew what this was about: Andrew. I had been friends with Andrew for a number of years. He and a good friend of mine had gone to college together, and we had all spent time together as we were starting to figure out this grown-up world. He was full of life and laughter and had a sharp wit. A few months before the healing workshop I was now in, he had been running in a race in Chicago. As he was running toward Soldier Field where the race ended, he collapsed and was never revived. He had a heart condition that he didn't know about, and he died right beside his father, who was running with him that day.

As the all-knowing eye continued to stare at me within, I felt rage, powerlessness, and sorrow. How could I love a God who was connected to the unfairness of death? I didn't want anything to do with Him. As I sat there, crying in frustration and sadness and feeling the pain of it all, I could feel a portal open. And there he was — Andrew. He was with me. He had come to tell me something. What was it?

"It is okay. I am okay."

The tears kept flowing, but they had less to do with fear and pain, and more to do with relief and gladness. He really was okay. I knew it was true. I didn't have to fear God; I didn't have to be afraid at all. After a little bit, Andrew faded from my vision, but I knew that he hadn't really left. He was still here with me. He always was.

Now I felt less fear and anger toward God, but knew I still had more to heal. This experience helped me understand that finding peace and love within myself depended on releasing pain and resentment.

Infinite Patience

Now you must learn that only infinite patience produces
immediate effects. This is the way in which time is exchanged
for eternity. Infinite patience calls upon infinite love, and by
producing results now it renders time unnecessary.
[Chapter 5, Section VI.12]

I DON'T have infinite patience! Most of the time I want things my way, and if I don't get them now, I can become upset. Now, since I'm a 'Nice Guy'™, I am not usually overt about all of this. I might be secretly upset, and behind my smiling face, I am grinding my teeth. My work with the Course has taught me how to be aware of this long-standing pattern, but to a certain extent, it continues to this day. This dynamic is beautifully illustrated in the section of the Course entitled "Self-Concept versus Self." Here, the concept of the "face of innocence" is introduced and elegantly explained:

"And so this face is often wet with tears at the injustices the world accords to those who would be generous and good. This aspect never makes the first attack. But every day a hundred little things make small assaults upon its innocence, provoking it to irritation, and at last to open insult and abuse."

[Chapter 31, Section V.3]

How many of us know this dynamic! It has helped me to see how insidious the ego can really be. Even when we're trying to be nice, oftentimes we are holding grudges in subtle or perhaps more obvious ways.

So, what's the solution? Deep and profound self-honesty. Letting ourselves uncover every piece of anger and fear and wring out every drop of shame within our minds. These energies are not truly at home there. We have inadvertently welcomed them in, and now it is time to gently and smoothly let these alien house-guests of shame and fear be witnessed and be gone. There need be no judgment, condemnation or anger directed at ourselves during this release. We can be compassionately kind and caring as we let the Spirit within sort out the true from the false. What is true is love, joy, peace and happiness — all that is real and eternal. We cannot lose this. What is the false, then? Everything else — pain, shame, bitterness, anger, frustration, and the like. As we allow the false to surface in our mind, we need not judge it. All we need do is witness it and when ready, watch it fade away. What remains is our eternal state as One with God. This state never changes or dissolves, although we may lose awareness of it.

"Forgiveness, on the other hand, is still, and quietly does nothing. It offends no aspect of reality, nor seeks to twist it to appearances it likes. It merely looks, and waits, and judges not. He who would not forgive must judge, for he must justify his failure to forgive. But he who would forgive himself must learn to welcome truth exactly as it is." [Workbook, Part II.I]

That becomes our whole work: welcoming truth. Again and again, we look at the log within our own eye, and only then we can help our brother with the speck in his.

I am learning this as I go, letting each grievance surface and asking for help to see it with eyes of love instead of judgment. One time, this happened very visually for me. I was going through a challenging time with my family. People who were dear to me were in conflict with one another, and I wanted everyone to get along. I was feeling powerless, and in a lot of hurt and pain. Even though I was trying to move through it and let it go, I was having trouble not feeling like a victim.

I visited an ACIM group that was led by my friend Lacey Whittington. During the group, she guided us into a meditation and I went very deep, soon seeing an image of all my family members and myself as puppets on a stage. Each puppet was acting out its familiar script, only now it all seemed absurd. I could see that each of the puppets was actually asking for love; all the hurtful words and actions didn't really add up to a hill of beans. There was nothing to them. I could feel myself being washed clean of my anger and bitterness. In reality I had never been hurt by them; in reality, nothing had happened; in reality there was truly nothing to forgive. Peace and freedom washed over me and cleansed all the false, painful thoughts within. I was able to rest in this peace, knowing I wasn't really a puppet in this drama of my life. As the Course taught me, I wasn't a body. I was free. For I was still as God created me. [Lessons 201-220]

This perspective would return to me again in new and different dramas. Each time it helped me unhook myself from the story playing out on the worldly stage, and realize I wasn't a victim. In fact, my mind was the puppeteer, and I could choose to wake up from this seemingly real show. This was freedom, and escape from madness. I counted my lucky stars that I had been given this wonderful teaching — a direct pathway home.

EXERCISE

Experiencing Non-Dualism

Let's try something. I'd like you to read each of the following forty sentences. You may want to skip over some but I encourage you to read all of them. Let's go!

This world is not real.
This world is not real.
This world is not real.
This world is not real.
This world is not real.
This world is not real.
This world is not real.
This world is not real.
This world is not real.
This world is not real.
This world is not real.
This world is not real.
This world is not real.
This world is not real.
This world is not real.
This world is not real.
This world is not real.
This world is not real.

This world is not real.
This world is not real.
This world is not real.
This world is not real.
This world is not real.
This world is not real.
This world is not real.
This world is not real.
This world is not real.
This world is not real.
This world is not real.
This world is not real.
This world is not real.
This world is not real.
This world is not real.
This world is not real.
This world is not real.
This world is not real.
This world is not real.
This world is not real.
This world is not real.
This world is not real.
This world is not real.
This world is not real.
This world is not real.

Wow! How do you feel? This may have brought up a lot of different emotions or experiences for you.

Now let's move on to what *is* real. Again, do your best to read all of the following sentences.

I am the Light of God.
I am the Light of God.
I am the Light of God.
I am the Light of God.
I am the Light of God.
I am the Light of God.
I am the Light of God.
I am the Light of God.
I am the Light of God.
I am the Light of God.
I am the Light of God.
I am the Light of God.
I am the Light of God.
I am the Light of God.
I am the Light of God.
I am the Light of God.
I am the Light of God.
I am the Light of God.
I am the Light of God.
I am the Light of God.
I am the Light of God.
I am the Light of God.
I am the Light of God.
I am the Light of God.
I am the Light of God.
I am the Light of God.
I am the Light of God.
I am the Light of God.
I am the Light of God.
I am the Light of God.

I am the Light of God.
I am the Light of God.
I am the Light of God.
I am the Light of God.
I am the Light of God.
I am the Light of God.
I am the Light of God.
I am the Light of God.
I am the Light of God.
I am the Light of God.
I am the Light of God.

How do you feel? Breathe and rest with whatever you're experiencing now. Just give yourself some time to feel what's happening. Feel free to put the book down to be fully with your feelings.

A Soul Reunion

*Those who are to meet will meet, because together
they have the potential for a holy relationship.*
[Manual for Teachers, Section 3.I]

UP AND UP we went. The spiraling path through the red rocks of Sedona led us along the energy of the vortex. I could feel the big energy here and its transformational power, even if I didn't know where it would lead. I went with the flow as the group of us climbed even higher. We turned a corner and were given yet another beautiful vista, an awesome scene that pulsed with a joyful beauty unlike any I had ever seen. We hiked up even further, coming to a large and relatively flat rock outcropping, where we gathered for another healing exercise. As we partnered up to begin the exercise on asking for what we want, my mind drifted back to Penny. She was smiling at me in welcome as I came in the door at the retreat house. My reaction to her when we first met was surprising.

"It's nice to see you. I'm glad you're here," I had said.

That wasn't a typical thing for me to say to someone I had just met. But it didn't feel like I was just meeting her; I felt like we had known each other a long time. It was a deep heart-based reunion. As I considered where this connection might be coming from, the facilitator's directions permeated my awareness, drawing me back from my reverie. I wasn't paired with Penny for this piece of the healing weekend but couldn't help notice her sitting with her partner for this exercise near us on the rock shelf. She was focused on the directions at hand. I took that as a cue to engage fully in the exercise and see where it led.

The whole weekend was amazing. The healing power of the area, and the compassionate instruction about opening spiritually through tantra were helping me to peel back whole layers of the ego within me. Tantra is a healing path that connects us to our true Self through healing and releasing blocks about sex so we can experience our full being. In order for us to heal all of what is within, we need to be willing to look at all that is within. And that includes sexuality and romantic partnering. Not all spiritual teachings touch on this topic, and the Course doesn't say much. But it does advocate leaving no stone unturned within us as we travel our spiritual quest. *"To learn this course requires willingness to question every value that you hold. Not one can be kept hidden and obscure but it will jeopardize your learning."* [Chapter 24, Introduction]

As the weekend unfolded, I shared my romantic feelings with Penny, and she expressed many of the same feelings back to me. I was elated! It felt like the beginning of a really good thing — both a budding romance and soul reconnection at the same time. She was a singer and I loved that about her. All kinds of things were clicking between us.

With the weekend retreat ending, Penny was staying in Sedona a few more days to experience more of the beautiful setting, and I was heading back home to Chicago. When she returned to Chicago, where she also lived, I knew we would get together.

However, excited as I was, it didn't go well. On that first get-together back in Chicago, I was flying high as a kite, just from the joy of it all, and it seemed like Penny was having a fun time as well. In this state of wanting to share everything with her, I shared a disturbing thought that had come up in me. An image had come into my mind of me raping her, and I told her this. I knew the image was coming up to be felt and released, so the emotions and issues around it could be undone, but I didn't explain that part of it very well. The issue of sexual assault had come up over the weekend as a part of her healing journey. It was something she had dealt with before. She was deeply upset and triggered by my sharing. It took her into a dark place. I had shown her one of the deepest, darkest thoughts within me on what was basically our first date.

She didn't want much to do with me after that, and I couldn't blame her. I had shared a dark shadow that wanted to be seen for healing, but in a way and context that wasn't safe or considerate of what she was ready for, or able to be with objectively. I think most people would end that connection if they were in her shoes.

I went through many months of healing and inner forgiveness work to release the blame I directed at myself for the way our time together had ended. It was amazing what highs and lows of emotions I had experienced when all of our interactions happened in about a week of time. You never know what opportunities for healing will come up, or how they will unfold. Now, with hindsight, I could see that all of it was an important healing lesson for me, even if that was sometimes hard to see while I was going through it.

A Life of Permanent Joy!

*And with each step in His undoing is the separation
more and more undone, and union brought closer.*
[Chapter 17, Section III.6]

A S MEMORIES of my past lives surfaced, I had to ask myself what they were for. ACIM suggests that everything we experience is to be forgiven, in order to awaken from the dream of this world to the truth of our eternal oneness with God. In Workbook Lesson 124, *"Let me remember I am one with God,"* the Course reminds us that when we are experiencing this truth, *"Everything we touch takes on a shining light that blesses and that heals. At one with God and with the universe we go our way rejoicing, with the thought that God Himself goes everywhere with us."*

So I could use these old memories and traumas and pains to wake up to the fact that however powerfully I felt them, the experiences were not my truth. They were simply momentary clouds covering the spiritual sun, keeping the love within from my conscious awareness. But with Spirit's help, I was getting better at moving through the clouds — to see them, but not *be* them.

Now, feeling and acknowledging pain, shame, and guilt is

rarely easy. These feelings are uncomfortable and may make us feel like we've done something wrong. No one likes to look at all the pain within, yet doing so is key to healing and release. Suppression, denial, and pretending that something false is true are more common strategies; most of us resort to them. We've all done our share of hiding. I do my share of it as well. Speaking of us as little children, the Course says: *"But if they hide their nightmares they will keep them."* [Chapter 12, Section II.4]

Why do we want to hold these sickly patterns close, hiding them from the light of healing even while they continue to be painful? Because doing so allows us to hold on to our belief in our individuality, and individuality is the opposite of oneness.

We think that letting go of individuality is going to be our end because the ego tells us that without it, we would be nothing. What we don't see is that without our seeming individuality, we would regain awareness of the formless infinity that we haven't really left in truth. This letting-go of our tiny self is one of the biggest challenges that every spiritual seeker faces. As we learn in the section titled "Self-Concept versus Self", the thing we think we are is not our truth: *"A concept of the self is made by you. It bears no likeness to yourself at all. It is an idol, made to take the place of your reality as Son of God."* [Chapter 31, Section V.2]

Without this false concept of our self, what would we really lose? With it goes all fear, shame, guilt, suffering, and pain. Without a belief in separation and its concomitant ideas of "otherhood" and being an individual, there actually is no pain. The clear message of the Course is that the only "sacrifice" of giving up our individuality is all the pain associated with it:

"Here will you understand there is no pain. Here does the joy of God belong to you. This is the day when it is given you to realize the lesson that contains all of salvation's power. It is this: Pain is illusion; joy, reality. Pain is but sleep; joy is awakening. Pain is deception; joy alone is truth. And so again we make the only choice that ever can be made; we choose between illusions and the truth, or pain and joy, or hell and Heaven." [Lesson 190]

A Life in Atlantis

Love has no darkened temples where mysteries are kept
obscure and hidden from the sun. It does not seek for
power, but for relationships. [Chapter 20, Section VI.4]

THE PAIN in my ear was not letting up. There was a tightness in the right side of my neck and into my ear that had crept up subtly over the last couple of weeks. Working on it myself, stretching, and trying other techniques had so far shown moderate but not permanent relief. The drops I put in my ear helped a little, but what would do the trick, and help this pain really go away? I wondered if my next workshop with Cindy would reveal what was going on.

As the morning of the workshop arrived, my neck and ear felt as bad as ever. Maybe I shouldn't go, I thought.

But when I tuned in, my inner guidance was a definite *yes* for attending. I knew I needed to go to the workshop. It would surely help.

When I got there, a few of the other participants had already arrived. This was a really good group of people — all healers, most with a psychotherapeutic background. Cindy had started this group to help those of us who wanted to deepen our healing abilities to use in our businesses.

After we had spent some time meditating and Cindy shared about what we would be working on that day, we jumped right in. She asked who would like to be the focus of some healing work. I didn't hesitate to raise my hand, and she smiled as she called on me, seeing my eagerness for the energetic shift that was about to unfold.

Cindy took the role of primary healer, instructing us on what she was doing as she went. She was modeling the healing technique, and at the same time, having everyone else in the circle practice healing focused on me. When she asked me what I would like to work on, the answer was clear and immediate: the pain in my right ear and neck. It immediately intensified when I named it. She had me name how it felt, so I described the pain. In the ear, it was an intense and very small area of pain, and it radiated down my neck and now even into my shoulder.

As the pain intensified, one of my fellow practitioners said that she could feel the pain as well, and that it was really a lot! As an intuitive, she was psychically picking up on my pain and experiencing it herself. Cindy encouraged her to pull her energy back, because as healers we need to observe clients' energies but not absorb them. But what was the cause of all this pain? I was gently encouraged to keep breathing with it and letting it unfold in my awareness.

Fragments of its source began to come into my mind. It had something to do with my intuition; somehow I was pushing my intuition away. It felt wrong, bad. The energies of shame and sorrow were present as well.

Then an image floated forward. I was a powerful, magical

woman. I saw myself wearing very fine clothes, elegant and beautiful. But there was a cruelness in me. Something in me looked hard as stone. I had misused my power. My natural intuition and sensitivity to the unseen had helped me move up the ranks in a spiritually advanced society, all the way to the level of a high priestess. But I had a deep dark secret.

In my studies, I had inadvertently discovered that there was a way to trap another's life force, which could then be used as I wished. I realized that I could use these powers to keep my body looking young. I could also use them to keep challenges to my authority at bay. I could bend some other people's wills to do what I wanted them to, politically, personally, even sexually. It was intoxicating, this kind of power. I took full advantage of this newfound ability to get what I wanted, even as I knew on a deeper level that it was wrong to do.

Then it hit me — all this was happening in Atlantis. I knew it as clear as day. A part of me protested, because I had never believed anything I heard about Atlantis before. It all sounded like a made-up myth to me. I couldn't believe that there was a spiritually and technologically advanced society living on an island in the Atlantic Ocean many thousands of years ago. But now I couldn't question it. The message was so clear. I also saw that the dynamic I was going through in my priestess past life — the need for power and control corrupting and disconnecting the internal link to Spirit — was a microcosm of the much larger version of this unfolding in the island paradise's tragic downfall.

I saw that I had manipulated and used almost everybody I knew in that lifetime. Of course I wouldn't want to connect more deeply to my intuition, after I had misused it so badly that time.

The pain was an energetic block in my ear — a big part of me was determined not to 'hear' these inner messages that I was intentionally seeking out by developing my intuition.

As it all came forward so clearly, the pain shifted. It became more diffuse, and then it started to lessen. The group of healers guided me to seeing that I didn't need to feel bad about what I was seeing. I wasn't making the same choice in this lifetime as I did before. I would be using my gifts this time for real healing, which inevitably leads to love-based connection — seeing we're all one. I could let the guilt go, melt away.

After this experience, the earache never came back as intensely again. Later, when I was healing other issues about my intuition, a mild version of the earache would come back, like a faint echo of the intense healing that happened here. Many if not all of our physical ailments, injuries, and illnesses are connected to unconscious traumas and unhealed memories. These traumas may originate in the life we're living now, but can also be connected to previous lifetimes. We can sometimes heal physical problems by undoing the underlying psychic wounds that we are carrying around in our everyday lives. This is the path to complete healing.

Discovering Real Kindness

That this is all the body does is true, for it is but a figure
in a dream. But who reacts to figures in a dream unless he sees
them as if they were real? The instant that he sees them as they
are they have no more effects on him, because he understands
he gave them their effects by causing them and making them
seem real. [Chapter 27, Section VIII.4]

M ANY experiences in my day-to-day life have strengthened
the idea that the world is not what it seems. Often it doesn't
seem real at all. The past life memories I have are compelling, but
not real either — at least, no more real than the life I think I'm
having this time around. The point is that all lifetimes, past, present and future, are simply dream experiences whose purpose is
to convince me that my perceived separation from God is real. As
I'm starting to get it, I'm taking the ego's bait less and less often.

Still, I struggle with this idea even as I learn more about it.
I don't want to relinquish the idea of my individual self; I'm quite
attached to thinking of myself as the person named Barret. Yet
I recognize that this individual, bodily identity is a trick I am
unconsciously playing on myself to blot out the reality of my
complete oneness with Love. It seems pretty effective too. When

the body seems to be experiencing pain, *I* feel like I am experiencing pain. When the body feels hungry, *I* feel hungry. When the body is sleepy, *I* feel tired. I unconsciously and strongly believe what the body feels is what I feel. The Course isn't asking me to deny my experiences in this bodily world, but helping me to see that they aren't ultimately true.

Why? Because nothing temporal is actually real. All our bodily experiences are nothing but a seemingly massive, long-lasting hallucination. Another way I'm learning to think of it is to realize that this is all an ongoing dream, and my job here is to wake up from it! ***"What if you recognized this world is an hallucination? What if you really understood you made it up? What if you realized that those who seem to walk about in it, to sin and die, attack and murder and destroy themselves, are wholly unreal?"*** [Chapter 20, Section VIII.7]

Well, this is all going to take some time, because as simple as these ideas are, I'm unconsciously terrified of where they are pointing. The Course's path of awakening is a gentle one, even in the face of my massive resistance. It is telling me I need only deal with what's in front of me at any given moment, and take everything one step at a time. That means applying these concepts to my day-to-day life, as well as any past lives that surface in my awareness.

As I study it, I have learned that the Course uses words like *fear* and *love* as bigger, more comprehensive terms than I was used to. These words represent two completely distinct thought systems that each of us is always choosing between. Fear, as it's used in the Course, covers the whole idea of separation, and the great variety of feelings that arise from the mistaken belief that it's real. Love is much more expansive as well; the Course sees love as pure, whole, unchanging joy and peace. It is the state of oneness with God, which is each of our eternal Truth now and always.

However, while a part of my mind is still attached to fear, I will unconsciously block myself from experiencing this peace. The work, then, is always to clean the spots of fear from the mirror within the mind.

"In this world you can become a spotless mirror, in which the Holiness of your Creator shines forth from you to all around you. You can reflect Heaven here. Yet no reflections of the images of other gods must dim the mirror that would hold God's reflection in it. Earth can reflect Heaven or hell; God or the ego. You need but leave the mirror clean and clear of all the images of hidden darkness you have drawn upon it." [Chapter 14, Section IX.5]

This work of cleaning my inner mirror is synonymous with forgiveness. I must forgive each and every grievance that I hold, turning it over to that higher wisdom within. The goal for my life then becomes reflecting the love of God in everything I do and every word I say.

EXERCISE

Attuning to Your Heart

How can you know whether you chose the stairs to
Heaven or the way to hell? Quite easily. How do you feel?
Is peace in your awareness? Are you certain which way you go?
And are you sure the goal of Heaven can be reached?
If not, you walk alone. Ask, then, your Friend to join
with you, and give you certainty of where you go.
[Chapter 23, Section II.22]

AWARENESS of what is happening within is a necessary part of our work with the Course. Do we feel happy, peaceful and light? Or something else? Bringing our experiences of tension and upset into the light is the beginning of healing them. This exercise is helpful in practicing inner awareness. Read through it once and then do your best with it.

Let your eyes gently close.

Take several deep and gentle breaths.

Let your mind's eye bring its focus to the area of the heart. Continue to breathe gently and notice what you find. How does your heart feel?

You may be noticing feelings or sensations of calmness and restfulness. Or memories may be surfacing. Sensations of tension, anger, or even boredom may be coming up. No matter what it is you're feeling, let yourself continue to gently breathe with it.

Stay in this place for at least a few minutes, perhaps even longer, being aware of what you feel in your heart and breathing.

When you are complete, thank yourself for bearing witness to your inner state. Extend gratitude to whatever you found within.

The Healing is Ongoing

Each small step will clear a little of the darkness away,
and understanding will finally come to lighten every corner
of the mind that has been cleared of the debris that darkens it.
[Workbook Lesson 9]

A S AN energy healer, I often receive treatments from other professionals. It is an important way to keep my energy as clean and clear as it can be for my clients and myself. It also helps me address any blind spots I have within my own mind and energy field, as well as difficulties that I'm having with self-healing.

I was working with Sharon Berkowitz as she led me through an experience of The Body Code™, a system that helps identify and resolve energetic issues in the body and the mind using muscle testing, also known as kinesiology. After I released several energetic blocks she commented, "When things like this come up for you in the future, you'll be able to handle them differently. You'll take a step forward, or backward, or move to the left or to the right. But it won't be the same stuck energy."

As she shared a little more about moving energy rather than remaining stagnant, I felt something stirring in me. I needed to move. The session was happening on the phone, so I got up from my chair and started walking around. I really felt like pacing, so I did. At some point, I felt like I wanted to shake my hands too. My phone was on a headset and wasn't in the way, so I did that too.

In the midst of this movement, I began feeling intense, overwhelming pain, sadness, and grief. Another past life was coming up: I could see that someone I knew had been killed or seriously hurt. I shared with Sharon, "I didn't do anything, and he died. It was a co-worker. He fell into a machine. If I had done something, maybe I could have saved him, but I didn't. I froze, and he died right in front of me."

I burst into tears. Why hadn't I done anything? He didn't have to die. The gory image of his death became clearer in my mind as intense feelings of sadness and remorse came up for healing and release in the form of big, heavy sobs.

The intensity of the memory didn't hang around for long, however. As the feelings continued to reveal themselves and then subside, the healing moved through quickly. This speed-up of the healing process was a cumulative effect of the countless layers of healing that had come before. It was clear to me that, as time went on, I was able to go just as deep in healing these issues as before, but the process was completing in less time. It also felt like I was achieving a "cleaner" shift, meaning that I fully released the issue and the accompanying emotions.

After the session was finished, I felt that something big had unfolded. How many times in my life had I experienced freezing up rather than moving forward, and all the anxiety around that dynamic? Having fewer of those feelings in the future was an amazing prospect. A wave of gratitude for all that was revealing itself swept through me, and settled onto my face as a big, happy grin.

The Reason for Healing

The real world is the symbol that the dream of sin and guilt is over, and God's Son no longer sleeps. His waking eyes perceive the sure reflection of his Father's Love; the certain promise that he is redeemed. [Workbook, Part II.8]

THE REASON for healing is release from pain. I think we all want that! I know I do, and that release from pain is the fuel that keeps encouraging me to study the Course. The idea of being pain-free, without suffering of any kind, is a powerful suggestion that there is much more to our existence than the regular experience of our day-to-day lives. The Course describes this way of life as seeing the "real world."

Being in the real world means experiencing this world of space and time with absolutely no belief in it, knowing that only what is changeless is real. When we have a dream in bed at night, it may be scary and very intense. If we realize in the dream that all of it is not real, our experience becomes dramatically different. The monster that is chasing us may turn into a little kitten, or we may start flying around! This experience of lucid dreaming, or knowing we are dreaming in the middle of it, is usually a very liberating and expansive realization. Awakening from the "daily dream" of fear to see that this physical world we are experiencing is also just a dream is no less liberating!

It is possible for us to experience this world as a lucid dream even as we go through our lives here. What are some of the qualities of living lucidly? Our awareness is very gentle and forgiving; there is a sense that nothing in the world can hurt us, or affect our real state of being. An all-encompassing sense of peace pervades our whole experience. Many other feelings or thoughts that reflect this right-minded way of being will arise as well.

After several years of practicing the concept of forgiveness in my life, I was blessed with a pretty remarkable experience of this way of being. It occurred after a seminar with Dr. Kenneth Wapnick, who is the premiere teacher of *A Course in Miracles*. Ken transitioned from the physical in 2013, yet I refer to him in the present tense because I know he is still here with me, gently encouraging me to remember that kindness is what I want. He is available to anyone who wants him as their guide.

I lived in California for about a year in 2009, during which time I finished writing my book, *Questions for J*, about my inner journey with the loving guide within. I was also able to attend a number of classes and seminars at Ken and Gloria Wapnick's Foundation for *A Course in Miracles*.

I was driving back home to the San Diego area from Temecula, where the foundation was located. Suddenly, everything I was seeing appeared to be a cut-paper animation. The hills in front of me, the road, the sky were all made of paper, moving just as they always had, but as paper instead of some solid substance. I continued to drive down the paper road, in my paper car, knowing that none of it was real. I was making it all up! And this was always the case, not just during this experience, but all the time.

All my worries and cares dissolved. How could I be concerned about something that wasn't real? There was absolutely no cause for fear. Nothing had ever happened; not really. Nothing had ever happened. I just kept driving, and eventually the experience faded from my perception. Everything seemed to resume its three-dimensional appearance. However, the massive *Aha!* connected to this perception would never leave me. I would never again look at the world in the same way. What a beautiful gift!

Letting Myself Love the Despised

If sickness is separation, the decision to heal and to be
healed is the first step toward recognizing what you truly want.
Every attack is a step away from this, and every healing thought
brings it closer. [Chapter II, Section II.I]

KEN WAPNICK taught me two words that are essential to experiencing the profound love that *A Course in Miracles* intends for us to know: "without exception." If I were to apply these teachings completely, I would forgive completely, and then love completely. I would hold no grievances — without exception. As the Course puts it, love requires the complete willingness *"to let forgiveness rest upon all things without exception and without reserve."* [Workbook, Part II.9]

I could see the logic in that. If we are all one, then every time I judge someone else, I am actually judging myself. Every time I hate, fear, or become angry about anyone, I am actually feeling all that about myself. This was a big realization for me; I couldn't believe all the awful things I had been delivering right back to myself for so many years. My whole life had been littered with grievances. I didn't think of myself as judgmental or angry, but I found plenty of ways to blame others. It was like I was throwing garbage out the driver's window of my car as I drove, but it all ended up in the back seat. No wonder my car stunk!

After a while, I understood how the Course was pointing me toward all-encompassing love. Yet, I didn't feel I could actually live it. I felt that I could be loving to the people in my life — my friends and family and people I knew. Even random strangers seemed easy to be kind and compassionate with. But there was one group I just couldn't stand: people who raped or abused children. They didn't deserve my sympathy; they deserved to be locked up, and to have what they did to the children done to them or worse.

Yet here was the Course, telling me that if I didn't extend love to them, then I was actually withholding it from myself. It felt like a square peg trying to go in a round hole. It just didn't fit. On one hand, I knew what the Course was telling me was true. But I could find no sympathy in my heart for these 'monsters.' So what could I do? I did my best to allow my feelings of disgust, and to practice forgiveness whenever I saw these situations on the news.

Then one day, I went to see a tantric sound and energy healer for a healing session. I had done trades with her that were very helpful, offering her my healing sessions in exchange for hers. I had released lots of pain and shame and false stories about myself, and had come into a truer sense of who I was. That day I was feeling fairly off, and felt like something big was going to come up in the session. The pattern of feeling upset, strange, or moody prior to a healing session was becoming clear to me. This out-of-sorts feeling usually preceded a big shift.

As the session got underway, I started to become sexually aroused. I got a bit embarrassed by the arousal, but then it became clear to me that this sexual energy was a part of the healing that was going to reveal itself. The session continued, and I began to get in touch with a sense of being sexually aggressive in a past life. I began to feel shame around this feeling, but I also knew that it was time to lift the veil and look at what had unfolded, so I kept going. My heart was pounding and my emotions were all over the place as the memories began to coalesce. Then I was there.

That little twat, she knew what she was getting herself into! And she wants to pretend now that she's not into it. Well she's going to get what's coming to her, I thought as I pressed myself onto a young girl who was twelve or thirteen years old. I was forcing myself on her while she resisted and pleaded with me to stop. But I couldn't hear her cries over the certainty in my head that she had tricked me into doing this. I was feeling victimized by her. I thought *she* had beguiled *me,* and I was powerless to stop it, all while I carried out this heinous act of rape. The rage and confusion in me were monumental. I was blinded by these intensely overwhelming feelings of sadness and shame that had morphed into aggression and rage.

As I came back from the past life memory, I was consumed with emotional pain and stunned disbelief. The awfulness of what I'd done was like a wraith that haunted me, condemning me. I allowed the grief, shame, and sadness to pour out of me in wave after wave of body-wracking sobs. It felt like a dam had burst inside me and the pent-up shame and sadness from this lifetime as a rapist kept flowing out of me, while the healer kept holding space for my pain. The tears flowed for a long time.

And then something occurred to me: I was innocent. In spite of everything I had just experienced, I was still innocent. As the Course shares with us, **"And he will look on his forgiveness** *there, and with healed eyes will look beyond it to the innocence that he beholds in you. Here is the proof that he has never sinned; that nothing which his madness bid him do was ever done, or ever had effects of any kind."* [Chapter 27, Section I.5] The teaching that the body is not real means that nothing anyone has ever done in this world has ever *really* occurred. There is no world to do it in, since all of this world is unreal.

Now I could see my anger at people who abused children lessening. I had been hating *myself* this whole time, but I wasn't able to see it until this experience unfolded. This helped me to see that I can't truly love if I am holding anyone apart from that love. That includes people who commit acts of rape, murder, torture, genocide and everything else. It includes *everyone.* I could see that this was a pretty tall order and would take a while to accomplish. But as my teacher Gary Renard said, "You've got nothing better to do." So true!

Let me be clear here: I am not condoning any acts of violence or suggesting those who break the law or hurt another should not have to deal with any consequences of their actions. Knowing everyone is innocent is a belief that goes beyond our physical forms to the truth of who we all are. In fact, it is possible to call the police or take action that causes someone to go to jail, all without any condemnation in our hearts or judgment of them as being somehow less than we are. In fact, this may well be the most loving and kind thing we can do for them, to end the cycle of punishment in which they are certainly trapped.

We Are Not Alone

Your Self-fullness is as boundless as God's. Like His, It extends forever and in perfect peace. Its radiance is so intense that It creates in perfect joy, and only the whole can be born of Its Wholeness.
[Chapter 7, Section IX.6]

CAN WE really comprehend that we are not alone? So much of our experience tells us otherwise. The circumstances of our lives show us all kinds of ways that we are alone; sometimes we can be in a crowd of people and still feel lonely. Because of this, we can see that feeling alone is not about whether other bodies are close by. It is actually a state of mind.

When I was a kid, if any of my siblings or I said that we were bored, my mom would tell us that being bored was a decision. We always had enough that we could do, and our feeling bored was not a reflection of reality but a decision to perceive our lives in a certain way. She was helping us to see that we could choose differently. Whenever she said this, it didn't take any of us very long to come up with something to do, and — *voila!* — the boredom was gone.

Similarly, any time we feel alone, we are actually making a decision (usually subconsciously) to believe that we are alone.

It's not a reflection of reality but just a decision to perceive our lives in a certain way. But it's possible to learn a better way of seeing things, that aligns us with our inner truth of connection and Divine Union.

This isn't easy, but it is something we can achieve. If we keep doing our inner healing work, the experiences of oneness, joy, and happiness are sure to follow. As we keep washing away the clouds, the sun is going to clearly shine! *"Yet the light is there. A cloud does not put out the sun."* [Chapter 29, Section VIII.3]

It's not always easy to be in the clouds. It can feel challenging, frustrating, and confusing. But as we read in the Course: *"Since all illusions of salvation have failed you, surely you do not want to remain in the clouds, looking vainly for idols there, when you could so easily walk on into the light of real salvation."* [Lesson 70] Here, we are reminded that being "clouded" is actually our choice, and we can make a new one any time we want. And it is said that we can "easily walk on," since walking through a cloud is not really hard. It is not like trying to walk through a wall.

One day, an opening in my inner clouds showed up for me. I was in a parking lot at a mall and had time before my next appointment, so I was just sitting in my car. It felt like a good time to meditate, so I did, and it was very nice. After I opened my eyes, I looked at the sky, and I felt the closeness of Love in a profound way. I knew I was never alone, that this big Love was as close to me as the sky. The sky is always there. Sometimes we call it air, and that's how close this big sense of Allness felt to me. Even though I was sitting in my car by myself, and there were no other people around, I knew so deeply that I was not alone, that I could not be alone. The very concept of being alone was impossible.

How amazing! I joyfully remained in that state of being as long as I could before I drove onward.

The World Is Not What It Seems

Let not the world deceive you. It was made to be deception.
Yet its snares can be so easily escaped a little child can walk
through safely, and without a care that would arrest its
progress. Dreams are dreams, and every one is equally
untrue. This is the only lesson to be learned.
[*The Gifts of God* by Helen Schucman, p.115]

THIS WORLD *seems* real. Sights, sounds, smells, tastes and touches seem to prove that there is a world here. The bodies we think we are appear quite real. But it's just not the case. This world is a massive subterfuge, hiding us from our reality. It is fed by our belief in the ego, but there is no inherent truth in it. **"Yet sights and sounds the body can perceive are meaningless. It cannot see nor hear. It does not know what seeing is; what listening is for."** [Chapter 28, Section V.4]

We are actually making up the senses that we experience as shields against knowing the divine Truth that we are. Why would we do that? Why would we make up a whole world to hide ourselves from God? Because we are unconsciously terrified of coming to know our unending connection with Oneness. We want to remain individuals and keep our separate identities. Just as there is no 'I' in *team*, there is no 'me' in *eternal oneness*. There is no Barret, there is no personhood. There is no 'other.'

"There is no statement that the world is more afraid to hear than this: I do not know the thing I am, and therefore do not know what I am doing, where I am, or how to look upon the world or on myself. Yet in this learning is salvation born. And What you are will tell you of Itself." [Chapter 31, Section V.17]

Our truth will be revealed to us as we allow Spirit to undo the false beliefs that we have about ourselves. This process may take a long time, which is why one of the characteristics of a good student is perseverance. I took Tae Kwon Do classes for a few years as a child, beginning at around six years old. There are five tenets of Tae Kwon Do, and *perseverance* is the third one. The last of the five is *indomitable spirit*. That is the attitude we develop as we heal and undo all the false thoughts, beliefs, and memories within ourselves. Another characteristic of the spiritual student is *integrity*. When we heal our false thoughts and beliefs, our internal consistency goes up. Another way to say it is that there is less about us that opposes the truth.

As I continued to ask for help with whatever issue was coming up for me, light was starting to shine through the veil of the physical world. Sometimes, actual sparks would light my vision, or little light orbs would dance around as I looked at the world. More often I simply sensed that some of my experiences were not real, which helped me not take things too seriously.

One day I was in my office, kneeling on the floor in meditation. When I opened my eyes, the floor in front of me was undulating like water. My first impulse was to shake myself out of it. But I got a nudge from within that this experience was a gift for me. So, I just watched the carpet move in a way that I knew was physically impossible. What became clear as I watched the carpet move in a wave-like manner was that *this world was actually impossible.* The carpet continued to undulate for a couple more minutes before this experience came to a close. Then I got up from my meditation.

I was beginning to comprehend what the Course teaches: ***"There is no world! This is the central thought the course attempts to teach."*** [Lesson 132] For most of us, these are just words. They may be hard to accept intellectually, or maybe not, but the unreality of this world is just a concept, a belief, an idea. But on a healing path, we will inevitably experience firsthand the dreamlike nature of this world. That is the answer to all our problems. We don't need to fix the countless, ever-shifting problems of the world. What we really need is to wake up from this dream of a world and remember the truth that is still within us.

This is not to say that there's nothing to do in the world. What matters is the motivation behind the actions we take. Are they coming from a need to fix a world that's going to eventually disappear from awareness, like rearranging the deck chairs on the Titanic? Or do we act to express our truth while we wake up to reality? It's the perspective that is important, not the specifics of what is unfolding on the level of form.

It actually doesn't matter what happens here in the world. Why is that? How much do the details of a dream you had in bed last night really matter once you awaken from the dream? Similarly, the details of this waking dream that we're experiencing don't really matter from the perspective of our eternal oneness. It's the love behind them that matters. It's always about the love.

EXERCISE

Listening to "Them"

A COMMON problem along the path of awakening is being stuck in an unhelpful thought pattern. This will sometimes involve a specific person about whom we have a grievance or judgment. How do we get out of this unhelpful thought pattern? This mental exercise may help.

Think of the person you've been having an issue with. You don't need to know them personally, but it's okay if you do. In your mind, surround them with a soft, white light. Let this light be with them as you gently breathe for a minute or more.

Tune in to what they want to say. Let them say it to you.

What did they say? Did you find it helpful?

Whatever it was you heard them say, let them go — gently into the light.

Making the Lemonade

And you will search for your home whether you realize where it is or not. If you believe it is outside you the search will be futile, for you will be seeking it where it is not. You do not remember how to look within for you do not believe your home is there. Yet the Holy Spirit remembers it for you, and He will guide you to your home because that is His mission. [Chapter 12, Section IV.5]

EVEN though the experience with the Landmark Forum in my twenties had been extremely disorienting, leading me to a psychiatric care facility, there were some genuine spiritual openings that resulted from their techniques. In retrospect, I was able to make lemonade out of the lemons that had showed up in my life. There is always a loving way to see what is unfolding in our experience, and in the past, if we are open to seeing it that way.

One memory stands out. After the event at Landmark, I had gone into a state of mind that was later diagnosed as mania. I felt very 'up' about my life, and everything had grand connotations. I thought I was going to save the world through Landmark techniques, and they were more than happy to have me recruit others to come to their introductory sessions. Not only did they openly encourage it, they also questioned seminar attendees who hadn't offered it to their friends and family yet. They wanted everyone to bring the people in their lives in, arguing that "If it has been so positive for you, why wouldn't you want the people you care about to experience this too?" I bought into this line for a while and promoted Landmark as a means to salvation.

But soon the whole thing soured for me. I could see the profit motive driving the organization more powerfully than the motive to help people. I felt that I had been conned, and meanwhile became somewhat socially erratic. It was like the doors to my sub-conscious storehouse of emotions and thoughts had been blown off their hinges. A lot of usually unspoken thoughts and feelings were just spilling out unfiltered.

During this manic period, I was driving very slowly in a snowstorm, hyper-alert to danger. It occurred to me that the snow on the hood and roof of my car was potentially unsafe; it could possibly blow up onto my windshield or onto a car driving behind me. I pulled into a gas station and began brushing off the couple inches of snow that had accumulated on my car. I was being very thorough about getting every last bit of snow off of my car, even in the middle of continuing snowfall. The gentleman parked next to me commented on what a thorough job I was doing; he probably sensed that something was off. But I took it as a compliment.

Toward the end of this task, I looked up into the sky and saw a bird flying through the snowfall, and deeply identified with it. The bird was flying home in the middle of the storm, and that's what I wanted so badly — to go home. I was deeply longing to be home with God, and it often felt like I was flying through the ongoing storm of life in order to get there. What I wouldn't grasp for quite a while is that the bird was *already* home in God, even as it was flying in the storm. And that was true for me as well; I was already at home in God, even as my dream experience was sometimes stormy and painful.

Thus I was just beginning to sense an inner wisdom that would guide me through storms. I was never alone, and even when the challenges of life seemed bereft of guideposts and trail signs, there was a presence within me that would help to lead me on. This presence is referred to as the Holy Spirit in ACIM; you might also call it the Higher Self, who knows the bigger picture and is there to help us through the bad weather of our lives.

"The Holy Spirit will always guide you truly, because your joy is His. This is His Will for everyone because He speaks for the Kingdom of God, which is joy. Following Him is therefore the easiest thing in the world, and the only thing that is easy, because it is not of the world." [Chapter 7, Section XI.I]

Everyone is Love

What God has willed for you is yours. He has given
His Will to His treasure, whose treasure it is. Your heart
lies where your treasure is, as His does. You who are beloved of
God are wholly blessed. [Chapter 8, Section VI.10]

AT ANOTHER of Cindy Libman's healing workshops, I experienced a healing that was profound and very insightful. We were again holding a healing space as a group for those who volunteered. I was generally very quick to say yes to these offers, because I knew the sense of freedom that these inner shifts would lead to. Cindy wouldn't always choose me in spite of my hand shooting up first, in order that everyone would have a chance to experience these group healing opportunities. But this time she did.

As I lay down on the cushion on the floor, the rest of the group gathered around me. Cindy guided us to a place of deeper centering within ourselves, as we collectively shared a brief time of silence. As the healing session began, I was led to name and bring forward the feelings, thoughts and sensations in me that were not at peace. I could feel the unease within me in the area of my heart and chest. I knew it was connected to the relationship

I was in at the time. I had been noticing the ways that I subtly sabotaged the relationship through irritation and upsets over seemingly trivial things. This was a part of a pattern that was both blatant and hidden at different times in my life, where I would hide from intimacy and closeness.

It seemed clear to me that the tension and upset in my heart was connected to this. Cindy encouraged me to go deeper into the experience. "What are you feeling? Describe it as fully as you can."

"I feel a tension in the area of my heart and chest. It feels heavy and stifling. I know I've been holding back from her. Finding faults in her over minor things," I shared.

"What are you experiencing now? Is it different in any way?" she asked.

"It now feels like a metal plate. A dark and solid plate covering over and protecting my heart. It's cold, but it's strong."

"What feelings are here?"

"Sadness. A feeling of isolation. Loneliness. But it's better than the alternative."

"What's that?"

"The alternative is crushing heartbreak." I broke into sobs. "The more I love her, the worse it is when it ends," I sputtered, as the tears kept rolling.

After I had cried for a while, and was starting to calm down, Cindy asked, "Is something happening that it will end? Are you uncertain about this relationship?"

"No, but sooner or later, one of us will die, and the thought of that pain is almost too much to bear. Oh my God!" Another fresh round of tears began to fall, as the group continued to hold a loving and healing space for this pain and sadness. The pain and awfulness of being without her was so frightening and intense that all I could do was let it up. It was too much to hold on to anymore. This wave of awful sadness just kept washing over me. With Cindy's help, I stayed with it as much as I could, letting it move through. At some point it started to become calm again within me. I felt like I had been washed clean of this unconscious burden I had been holding onto.

"What are you noticing now?" asked Cindy.

"Lightness. Presence. A shiny, sparkly feeling. There's a real feeling of light and joy in my heart. I feel like I can love her without all that fear. And there's more. In my mind's eye, I can see this amazing treasure chest in the area of my heart. This treasure chest is filled with beautiful gems; they're the most beautiful gems I've ever seen. Each gem is a person in my life — family, friends, each of you — everyone I know. You are all so dear to me, so valuable! I love you all so much."

This time the tears that fell were tears of joy and happiness. I felt like such a rich man right then — rich in love, richly connected to all of these people in my life. The old stuck sensations I had been having had covered this amazing light and happiness within me. I didn't even realize I could feel this much love. What a blessing!

All Paths Lead to Heaven

*Although Christian in statement, the Course deals with
universal spiritual themes. It emphasizes that it is but one
version of the universal curriculum. There are many others,
this one differing from them only in form. They all lead to
God in the end.* [Preface — What It Is]

BEFORE I became a student of the Course and its teachings,
I spent several years tuning into my intuition, cultivating
a connection to the inner wisdom that we all have. I developed
some skill in asking for guidance and feeling which options were
best. I can see now that I was loosening my grip on living life based
on what I thought was right, instead turning it over to a greater
power within. This is the Self that knows all things and is beyond
the limited ego self with which we identify most of the time.

"*In order to judge anything rightly, one would have to
be fully aware of an inconceivably wide range of things; past,
present and to come. One would have to recognize in advance
all the effects of his judgments on everyone and everything
involved in them in any way. And one would have to be certain
there is no distortion in his perception, so that his judgment
would be wholly fair to everyone on whom it rests now and*

in the future. Who is in a position to do this?" [Manual for Teachers, Section 10.3]

I found that trusting spiritual intuition revealed to me which trainings would be useful on my healing path, and which practitioners it would be good for me to learn from. I could even use it for simple things, like asking which way was the best route to drive home, if I had remembered to pack everything when going on a trip, or which spice would be good in the dish I was cooking. This inner asking became more and more a regular part of my decisions through the day.

However, there were times when I would get answers I didn't want to follow. If I was resistant or fearful about some intuition I was getting, I would often override the inner knowing, and do it my way instead. In hindsight it usually became clear that it would have been better to follow the inner directions I had been given. Other times, I never saw what I had missed out on by not being willing to take the encouraged path.

Sometimes I would be led to specific healing workshops or events that didn't necessarily have to do with what the Course was teaching. In these instances, I usually felt that there was some connection or purpose behind attending the event, and that it would be helpful on my healing journey. One of these occasions was with an event called The Grail — a men's healing retreat weekend that was led, interestingly enough, by women. It was a deeply healing experience for me, helping me to let go of large and heavy inner blocks that I was only somewhat aware of. I describe some of what unfolded at the retreat and afterwards in my first book, *Questions for J — And the Love that He Gave Me*. In addition to the three-day weekend, the members of this community also got together for circles that would last a few hours long.

It was during one of these circles that I got deeply in touch with a sense of intense anger and rage. We were encouraged to speak using "I-language:" phrasing like "I feel..." rather than "You know how you feel when..." in order to help us be present with what we were experiencing. We were also reminded to keep our sharing in the present moment and not dwell on what had happened in the past. In the days leading up to this circle, I had noticed myself becoming quicker with a sharp comment; it seemed as if something was brewing in me. Looking back at this time, I can see that my passive-aggressive tendencies were more prominently on display. A lot of it was directed at my girlfriend at the time; my ego patterns tended to show up most often in a romantic relationship.

In that moment, in a circle of men, the rage within began to come out. Rage about not getting my way, about feeling disrespected, about the sense of powerlessness in my life. Rage, rage, rage! It felt like an inner flood that was breaching the walls I had built to hold it back. I felt the urge to scream, so I did. It felt good to let it out, as if I was unburdening myself through this authentic expression that had been deeply repressed. My brothers in the circle simply witnessed and allowed. In this space, there was nothing I needed to do with what I was feeling. I didn't need to fix it, make it right, apologize for my anger, or feel that anything was wrong about it in any way. It was such a deep relief.

I had let go of an overwhelmingly intense layer of emotions, and gladly so. Healing the anger and rage inside me meant that I would never have to go through that part of it again. There would be other layers, but each one I healed lightened my unconscious load of repressed issues as I journeyed forward. Reminding us of this undoing, the Course says: *"Every chance given him to heal is another opportunity to replace darkness with light and fear with love."* [Chapter 14, Section III.6]

Getting Better Vision

*You want to see the sunlight and the glow of Heaven
shining on the face of earth, redeemed from sin and in the Love
of God. From here is prayer released, along with you. Your wings
are free, and prayer will lift you up and bring you home where
God would have you be.* [Song of Prayer, Section 2.II]

WHEN I was eleven years old, my teachers noticed that I
had started to squint when I was looking at the black-
board while sitting at my desk in class. They shared it with my
parents. Not long after, I was at the eye doctor, doing my best to
read the increasingly small and fuzzy letters on his vision chart.
Soon enough, I had my first pair of glasses, at the ripe old age of
eleven. It wasn't always easy — I heard my fair share of "four-
eyes" and the like from kids at school — but for the most part,
wearing glasses wasn't much of an issue for me.

It wasn't until much later in my life that I realized there were
underlying reasons behind this loss of acuity in my vision. I was
receiving a healing session on the phone when the topic of my
eyesight came up.

"What was happening in your life around the time you got
your first pair of glasses?" the healer asked me.

"I'm not sure," I replied.

"Let yourself feel into it. Are there any thoughts or feelings that you notice?"

I took a deep breath. As I focused in, I noticed something. "There's a feeling of sadness."

"Alright, stay with that feeling."

I let myself keep breathing and feeling this sadness. Another feeling came up. "Now I'm feeling like I don't want to keep looking at this. A part of me doesn't want to go there."

"So we're talking about lack of vision, and now you're telling me that there's something within you that you don't want to see. Probably not a coincidence," she said.

Her words really rang true. Something within was hiding from being seen, and somehow it was connected to my vision loss. Now the sadness was increasing. All of a sudden, I knew what was being hidden: the pain I hadn't fully felt around my grandmother's death. She had died at that time in my life, and a part of me didn't want to see the sadness and sorrow I felt about her loss. In that moment, I let myself cry, feeling even more fully the emotions I hadn't or couldn't let myself have when I was young. The tears flowed freely, carrying with them the grief over my grandmother's transition.

I hadn't known what to do with my sadness when I was a child, and the emotions had been on hold for all those years — under the surface but not gone. The inner hiding was the same as not seeing, and at least for me, had shown up on the physical level as diminished eyesight. As the healing call came to a close, I thanked her for helping me to see what was going on within me. I felt much lighter and freer! Even though I had heard about people's eyesight improving significantly after energetic shifts like this one, even to the point of not needing glasses anymore, this didn't happen for me. I was disappointed. I had hoped that one of these healing shifts would improve my eyesight so I wouldn't need glasses anymore. After months of hoping, I was starting to let go of thinking my vision would improve.

Then one day, a thought occurred to me. I would get corrective eye surgery. So I found an eye doctor, and underwent photorefractive keratectomy, a laser eye surgery, which made my vision better than 20/20. It wasn't the way I thought I would achieve better vision, but it was perfect for me. It was another example for me that when we let go of our conscious idea of how our life should go, our intuition can guide us on the path that's best for us.

"The images you make cannot prevail against what God Himself would have you be. Be never fearful of temptation, then, but see it as it is; another chance to choose again, and let Christ's strength prevail in every circumstance and every place you raised an image of yourself before. For what appears to hide the face of Christ is powerless before His majesty, and disappears before His holy sight." [Chapter 31, Section VIII.4]

An Experience of the Great Rays

The fact that God is Love does not require belief, but it does require acceptance. It is indeed possible for you to deny facts, although it is impossible for you to change them. If you hold your hands over your eyes, you will not see because you are interfering with the laws of seeing. If you deny love, you will not know it because your cooperation is the law of its being.
[Chapter 9, Section I.II]

EVERYWHERE I looked was an amazing, beautiful light. The walls were made of light, and the floor was the same light. Everyone and everything still had the shape they had before, but instead of skin and clothes, metal and fabric, all I saw was light! I was awestruck by this vision; it felt so new and also somehow more real than the way my eyes normally worked.

This remarkable experience occurred at an event I attended to deepen my intuition. The workshop was taking place in a hotel conference room, and the space was very clean and had a nice feeling to it. I arrived a bit early, checked in, and went to take my seat in one of the chairs in front of the stage. I was fairly new to this whole world of healing and intuition, and I didn't recognize anyone that I knew. I made a point of sitting beside an empty chair. I had quite a bit of nervous anticipation and didn't want to chat much with anyone before the workshop started.

As we got underway, I started to loosen up and enjoy the exercises we were guided through. The facilitator had a musician sharing his songs as the event went on, which helped to keep the atmosphere light and playful. In one of the first exercises, she told us to write "My soul is..." on a piece of paper and then continue writing, letting our words be a pure expression from our hearts. I enjoyed the process, and really got into writing a poem that was a genuine sharing of my soul. When everyone completed their writing, we handed our papers to her.

A pattern emerged during the weekend. After each break, the facilitator would start by reading a poem picked from the pile, "My soul is ..." Every poem was touching; sometimes they were fun or funny, other times they were sweeping and expansive, or mystical. Each was like a precious work of art. She never read the person's name, so it often left me wondering who had written it, impressed that this anonymous, amazing soul was here in our group.

Often, after reading one of these wonderful poems, she would say, "Did you see that? Did you see this soul when you walked in this morning? Did you see this?"

And my answer was inevitably: No. On the second day, when she shared another soul-revealing poem, something within me was ready for a shift.

"Did you see this? Did you see this soul?" she asked, and I broke down in tears. The fact that I hadn't immediately seen the beauty of this poem within one of my fellow participants shook me. Here I was sitting on my chair, surrounded by a hundred other people, and I had been unable to see what really mattered in everyone else because I had been so distracted by my own thoughts and problems. I didn't want to keep living like that. I wanted to open myself up to knowing the poetry inside everyone.

That's when I looked around me and saw everything and everyone made of light.

The illumination was stunning, and so new. My sadness gave way to awe, as I sat there wonderstruck by this vision of light. I allowed this new way of seeing to reveal to me that everything was not how it had always seemed to be. Amazement and joy continued to wash over me even as the vision of light began receding. The solid, physical world that I was used to reappeared, but knowing that the light was reality stayed with me. It was like a veil had briefly fallen from my vision, and I would never believe in the veil as much again. I felt so blessed and grateful that this experience had unfolded for me. What a gift!

"This world of light, this circle of brightness is the real world, where guilt meets with forgiveness. Here the world outside is seen anew, without the shadow of guilt upon it. Here are you forgiven, for here you have forgiven everyone." [Chapter 18, Section IX.9]

Our Eternal Innocence

*Here is the new perception, where everything is bright
and shining with innocence, washed in the waters of forgiveness,
and cleansed of every evil thought you laid upon it. Here there is
no attack upon the Son of God, and you are welcome. Here is
your innocence, waiting to clothe you and protect you, and
make you ready for the final step in the journey inward. Here
are the dark and heavy garments of guilt laid by, and gently
replaced by purity and love.* [Chapter 18, Section IX.9]

T HE WAVES lapped gently against the side of the ship as we
began to pull out of port. I gazed out at the horizon at the
open water of the Atlantic. This had been a good idea; I could
feel it in my bones. This cruise was organized by Hay House,
the biggest and most well-known publisher of spiritual books in
the world. I would be benefitting from the wisdom and insights
of four different spiritual authors, some of the top intuitives and
mediums in the country. As the ship powered out into open sea, I
could tell that I was moving into some deep water on my spiritual
path as well.

I was at an author's presentation when something triggered
a massive healing shift in me. This author was a medium, which

meant that he could access someone's loved ones who had crossed over and share messages from them. He asked that when he started doing a reading, we should raise our hand if what he was naming applied to us. That helped him to locate who the message was intended for. He suggested that it was important for us to listen to his readings as though what he was saying was for us, even if he was reading for someone else. Some of what he was saying could very well be for us all. I figured I would do my best to keep my ears open.

I didn't have much expectation that he would have a message for me. I didn't feel a strong need to hear from anyone, although a few of my grandparents had transitioned. Thus it was very unexpected when he said something that really stood out for me.

"I'm picking up on something to do with cemeteries," he said from the stage. A number of hands went up in the audience.

"Could be something to do with burials, maybe even someone involved in helping to bury people." A few of the hands started to go down.

"I'm getting an image of a tombstone falling over." His words surprised me. That connected for me. I raised my hand, feeling flushed and embarrassed.

"It's definitely a loved one who was connected to a cemetery, and maybe worked there." That wasn't me; I lowered my hand. He soon found the audience member whose father had been an undertaker and began letting her father's words come through for her. It was again very clear that it was helpful to her, and very healing to get this message from her father through the medium.

The reading wound down and the session ended. As we started to leave the auditorium, it suddenly hit me; his reading for her had nothing to do with a tombstone falling over. That part was just for me. When I was in high school, I had been running through a cemetery with some friends, and I had exuberantly decided to jump off a low-lying upright headstone. Rather than supporting my weight, it had tipped over. Mortified, I tried to tip it back up, but it was too heavy. I called one of my friends over, and we managed to get it back up to its original upright position. I couldn't believe what I had done and told no one about it.

As I walked out of the auditorium, a message of the Course came through for me: There was no cause for fear. *"What could you not accept, if you but knew that everything that happens, all events, past, present and to come, are gently planned by One Whose only purpose is your good?"* [Lesson 135] Suddenly I had a sense of never being alone, and being held in loving regard at all times.

I went back to my cabin, and the depth of this love and acceptance moved me to tears. I felt so loved, so held, so safe; it was awe-inspiring. I thought back to a few past-life experiences that had recently come up for me — lifetimes where I had been violent and attacking, hateful and vicious — and the love embraced me in them too. I wasn't really alone in those moments, even though I had felt that way at the time. I wasn't really ever alone. God was always with me, which meant love was always there. The shame and sorrow I had from those past-life choices could be let go. Wave after wave of old, shameful lifetimes surfaced so that I could lay down the painful traumas associated with them. I cried for a long time until I emerged into a feeling of being inside a soft and safe cocoon. I knew that this path was leading me home, step by step. I happily let myself drift off to sleep in my bunk with a gentle smile on my face.

A Note of Grace

Defenses that do not work at all are automatically discarded.
If you raise what fear conceals to clear-cut unequivocal
predominance, fear becomes meaningless. You have denied
its power to conceal love, which was its only purpose.
[Chapter 12, Section I.9]

"MORE HEIGHT! A taller sound!" said Carl, the conductor. He was staring right at me, as he motioned for me to "shape" my sound in the way choir singers are encouraged to vocalize. I felt my face flush with embarrassment. I had just joined this chorus, and was enjoying it for the most part, but the conductor's persistent comments and encouragements, though well-intentioned, were definitely getting under my skin.

"You don't want to spread the sound sideways, but up and down. Aim for a vertical space instead of horizontal."

The instruction was clearly meant to help us produce a better, more consistent sound as a group. Yet I was taking it very personally, feeling rather miffed and singled out, like he was putting me down. I knew that part of it was that I was one of the stronger male singers in this chorus, so my voice tended to stand out more than the others. This actually was an aspect of my singing that I could improve.

But after a couple of rehearsals with multiple suggestions about this issue, I found myself getting hot under the collar. It finally dawned on me to ask myself, "What is this for?" As the Course says, *"In any situation in which you are uncertain, the first thing to consider, very simply, is 'What do I want to come of this? What is it for?'"*[Chapter 17, Section VI.2]

I knew that the answer could be peace, and that's what I ultimately wanted. Why, then, was this irritating me so much?

It certainly seemed like it was connected to Carl. Other conductors in other choirs had made similar suggestions, and they would bother me a little, but not to the same degree. When I had some time, I let myself go into the feelings more deeply. As I tuned in to my experience, I encountered a rush of feelings: anger, upset, frustration. There was a sense of pushing against someone else. This anger felt like it had a focus, and the focus was a particular person. Another scene opened up within, and I went into it.

Where was he? Why could he never be on time? If he didn't show up soon, we would just have to start without him. Dammit! I started to prepare the rest of the military marching band to play the set without him. I was pissed. No one else could play the trumpet solo like he could; we didn't have a replacement. The show had to go on. It didn't matter if he was the best trumpeter in the whole army — this just would not stand. I was going to have to demote him out of the band. *Aaaughhh!* I screamed inwardly in frustration, as I gritted my teeth even harder.

Then, with just seconds to spare, there he was, tucking his shirt into his pants with one hand, and carrying his horn in the other. I glowered at him as he did his best to avoid my gaze.

"See me afterwards, private." We locked eyes for a second, as my strong upset was silently communicated. "Alright, let's go!" I called out to the band, as we headed out in formation.

The memory started to lessen, and I knew deep down that this had happened many times. Sometimes Carl had pushed me around, other times I had been the aggressor in a variety of scenarios. In that lifetime, I had been in authority over him, but there were others that mirrored my experience this time, where he was the leader. We had gone back and forth in many lifetimes, playing different sides of the coin, working through the karma and either deepening the aggressive pattern or beginning to heal it.

My anger at him in the present time was not really about the singing instruction, it was mostly about these deeper, painful issues within. This pervasive pattern could be witnessed and let go. I went through the forgiveness steps in my mind. I was projecting my anger and upset onto the situation. The dynamic with Carl was not really the source of my lack of peacefulness. As I brought the emotions back within, I could see that there was no real source for them within either. Why? Because all of this — the past life trauma and the current situation in the choir — was not true. It was just one massive illusion that I had cooked up to keep God's love away from me. Since none of it was real, I didn't need to suffer from it. I did my best to let it go and ask Spirit for help in seeing all of this with a loving perspective. *"Those who forgive are thus releasing themselves from illusions, while those who withhold forgiveness are binding themselves to them. As you condemn only yourself, so do you forgive only yourself."* [Lesson 46]

I could feel my sense of grievance lessening as I thought about these ideas from the Course. This forgiveness stuff really worked! I found myself being more peaceful and less stuck in the ideas and feelings of the ego — fear, judgment, separation. When Carl would make the same suggestions in later rehearsals, I found myself feeling less angry or hurt. Sticking with forgiveness and using it each time I thought of myself as a victim really helped me feel better as the choral season went forward.

EXERCISE

Coming Into The Body

AS WE study the Course lesson *"I am not a body. I am free. I am still as God created me"* [Lessons 201-220], it may seem counterintuitive to pay closer attention to what is happening in our bodies. However, healing and releasing all of our fears, judgments and upsets is exactly what practicing *A Course in Miracles* is about. Becoming more fully aware of what is happening in our bodies often brings these dark energies into the light where the undoing of fear occurs. This exercise will help you do just that. Let yourself read through the steps, then close your eyes and go through them as best as you can.

You can do this exercise sitting cross-legged or sitting in a chair. You can also do it while lying down, although a seated position may prevent falling asleep if you are tired.

Allow twenty minutes for this exercise if you can, although a shorter time is better than none at all.

With your eyes gently closed, take a few breaths and let yourself come fully into the present moment.

Let your inner focus move to the top of your head and rest there. Tune in to feel whatever sensations or feelings arise.

In a relaxed manner, let your inner focus move to the rest

of your scalp, forehead, and temples. Continue to your eyes and nose, cheeks and mouth, ears and jaw, then your chin. As you go from place to place within your mind, attend to whatever sensations or feelings you find in each place. If you find tension or unease somewhere, simply breathe with it a bit longer, and perhaps ask what it has to show you.

In your mind's eye, move onto the neck and shoulders, then the arms, wrists, hands and fingers, again resting wherever something comes up for your attention. Continue to breathe gently as you go.

Focus now on the upper chest, upper back, and shoulder blades, then the ribcage and spine. Breathe slowly from your abdomen while moving your attention to the stomach, navel and pelvis. Continue to shift your awareness downward, to the buttocks, anus and genitals. Let yourself be kind with whatever you find as you go. Inwardly witness this all with compassion.

Now move down the upper legs, knees, shins and calves, then ankles and feet including the heels and toes. Continue to spend more time with any tension or pain experienced anywhere.

Now turn your mind's focus to the entire body, gently and deeply breathing as you witness your whole physical experience. When you feel ready, let yourself gently open your eyes and come back into your surroundings.

If you are still noticing any upsets or discomfort after the exercise, please use the forgiveness thought process detailed earlier in the chapter "The End of Suffering" to continue to work through what you're experiencing.

Solar Campfire

Here is belief in differences undone. Here is the faith in differences shifted to sameness. And here is sight of differences transformed to vision. Reason now can lead you and your brother to the logical conclusion of your union. [Chapter 22, Introduction]

WE WERE sitting around the campfire as night began to settle in. The trees nearby provided comfort and a sense of stability, as well as a certain amount of protection from the breeze, although it wasn't blowing very hard that night. Our day of healing, dancing, meditative hiking and more had been great, and now we were gathering to enjoy some company. This year, my friend Jason and I had created our own retreat devoted to playfulness and inner journeying, attended by a half-dozen people.

We had led the group on a do-it-yourself exercise of making homemade instruments earlier that day. There were rattles made with peas or gravel in cardboard tubes, drums made from coffee cans and pie tins. Each of them was decorated with paints and colors and glitter, allowing us all to tap into the joyful and creative nature of our inner child. We all had a great time 'making music' and expressing ourselves.

An impromptu drum circle began as the evening sky

darkened, and the pops from the fire danced up towards the stars, as though they were calling out to their friends. The rhythmic pulse of the sound connected to something deep within me, and I arose to my feet. As I continued to play my drum with the others, I started to march around the campfire. A chanting emerged from my lips in tune with the drums. A few others from the group began to march and dance around the fire.

As we continued to step and sing and play our instruments, I found myself starting to go into a parallel but deeply inward experience. I was connecting back to many other lifetimes where I had been involved with a ritual or celebration around a fire.

The energy of this past-life review was like being led down a long hallway. Rooms on either side revealed to me other lives where I had also been by a fire, and I experienced a taste of each. There were the times when I had just watched, and times where I had been singing or drumming. But the lives where I was dancing or walking around the fire drew me in most of all. I knew as I stepped around the fire in this place and time that I was mirroring the same steps and movements from hundreds or thousands of years in the past. Time didn't feel like such a fixed and steady process; it was amorphous and multi-directional.

The genders and races that I experienced in these lifetimes were not important characteristics. I felt connections even beyond this planet, to other lifetimes celebrating events around fires while circling around other stars. Those lifetimes' bodies didn't look like the bodies we know, yet this ancient fire-ritual experience was familiar. The expanded, multi-planetary cosmic connection linked me to many varied experiences I had lived. I realized that I was not a specific, time-bound body.

"Only joy increases forever, since joy and eternity are inseparable. God extends outward beyond limits and beyond time, and you who are co-creator with Him extend His Kingdom forever and beyond limit." [Chapter 7, Section I.5]

As this multi-phase experience began receding, the present march around the fire was winding down as well. The rhythm of the drums was slowing and so was the dance. As I sat down on the log by the side of the fire once again, I felt different. All my daily problems and issues seemed fleeting and temporary; perhaps they had just been put into proper perspective. We played some more music and reveled in the joy of the fire. Soon I shared some of my experience with the others. The words I used didn't feel grand enough to fully convey the opening I had gone through, but the smiles on the faces of Jason and our companions suggested that they were getting a sense of it anyway. I was so grateful for all the healing we were going through!

Out of This World

Many holy instants can be his along the way. A goal marks the end of a journey, not the beginning, and as each goal is reached another can be dimly seen ahead. [Psychotherapy, Section 3.II]

As I progressed along my spiritual path with workshops, retreats, and reading, the topic of extra-terrestrial worlds and species kept coming up. Again and again, the message was: we aren't alone here. The idea isn't implausible is it sounds; out of two trillion or more galaxies, each with billions of potentially habitable planets, could we be the only sentient species of life that has developed? That seems more implausible to me.

The idea that all our past lives are not necessarily on one planet was mind-blowing at first. But I knew it was true as soon as I heard it. My first lifetime was not on Earth. When and where it was exactly seemed shrouded in a misty and unclear part of my mind; when I tried to tune into it, it seemed mostly unimportant. The healing work I have been involved in around past lives has always been about clearing karma, referred to in the Course as "unconscious guilt," which is always traceable back to the unreal belief that we have seemingly separated ourselves from our Source. My feeling about this first incarnation, so many lifetimes ago, was that there was no more karma associated with it. I had done the healing work for all the issues in that life.

As I explored this idea further, I developed a sense of how a soul's path typically unfolds. A soul stays on one planet, perhaps even as a member of one species, for a series of incarnations before moving on to another place. So we generally spend dozens or even hundreds of lifetimes on one planet or as one type of being before making a cosmic leap between incarnations to another planet. Some people may have made this leap a few times on their soul's path, but most of us have done this dozens or even hundreds of times. That's quite a trip!

Many people I've helped with healing work don't feel at home on this planet. Maybe they don't know how to get along with people, or they struggle with fitting into society's expectations, or they're challenged by the survival issues of health or money. In their healing sessions, an extraterrestrial past life may be recalled, in which the conditions of existence were so different that human ways of relating and surviving feel awkward and exceptionally challenging. Allowing the contrast to be acknowledged is a help-ful step on their journey to a deeper sense of ease with life. We're all looking to go home.

Yet none of the planets we may have inhabited in any of these lifetimes — tens of thousands for most of us — have ever actually been our home. We've never been at home in any of these dream lifetimes, because they are not true. It can be helpful at times to look at them, but only for the purpose of healing. Again, as the Course says about the universe of space and time: *"What if you recognized this world is an hallucination? What if you really understood you made it up? What if you realized that those*

who seem to walk about in it, to sin and die, attack and
murder and destroy themselves, are wholly unreal? Could you
have faith in what you see, if you accepted this? And would you
see it?" [Chapter 20, Section VIII.7]

Our task is not just to understand this idea intellectually, but
experience it fully. How do we do that? Step by step, simply by
forgiving whatever shows up in front of our faces or within our
minds day by day, minute by minute. We don't even need to have
any conscious awareness of past lives to heal all our unconscious
guilt. Everything that we need to heal will eventually show up in
our lives and self-awareness because the outer world is actually a
projection of the inner mind.

Increasingly I see that these long-ago and faraway lifetimes
are showing up in my awareness because I am ready to heal them.
With each one, I simply do my best to complete the process,
knowing that this is the route to a deeper sense of peace.

A Gentle Journey Home

Creation's gentleness is all I see. I have indeed misunderstood
the world, because I laid my sins on it and saw them looking
back at me. How fierce they seemed! And how deceived was
I to think that what I feared was in the world, instead of
in my mind alone. [Lesson 265]

As I continued living *A Course in Miracles*, I recognized an attitude of gentleness woven into its teachings. In fact, there are almost no proscriptions about behavior within the Course. Its clear message is that it's how we look at things that matters, not what we do. Practicing this principle day in and day out helped to shine light on some of my darker and unloving interactions with friends and family. I could see all the times that I thought I was being kind when my ulterior motives were actually at play.

A lot of people struggle with recognizing how the ego takes the reins in our relationships. Most of us see ourselves as good people, and any contrary information threatens our personal worldview. Once I saw what I was doing, I was often tempted to blame myself for the selfish actions I had taken and the unkind words I had said. I was learning, however, that attacking myself after the fact was yet another facet of the ego. I didn't need to double down on the unkindness by also being unkind to myself. Forgiving myself for the times I was expressing lack of love was just as important as forgiving others.

In the ego's worldview, unkindness has a sickly sweet payoff. It reminds me of the times I binge-eat candy or cookies. I feel compulsively like I want more, and more, and more. The sweetness of the food gets mixed with a feeling that's both physically and psychologically sick. Mixed in with the desire to overeat, or any other addictive problem that people experience, is an unconscious feeling of guilt and shame. As the Course puts it: *"If you did not feel guilty you could not attack, for condemnation is the root of attack. It is the judgment of one mind by another as unworthy of love and deserving of punishment."* [Chapter 13, Introduction]

I am just as good at judging another as I am at judging myself. As time unfolds I am seeing more clearly that it isn't worth the 'payoff.' I don't really want to end up in this sickly sweet kind of place. What I want is the clean and pure love of everyone, and that includes myself!

Laying down the sword of condemnation and attack is the outcome of this deepening dedication to a kind and gentle life. It reminds me of the medieval story of Parsifal, a knight who was determined to win every battle and best every opponent. And he did. Every foe was vanquished; everywhere he went, he ended up victorious. However, all these battles took their toll. The years of conflict wearied his body, mind, and spirit. He was deeply drained even as he continued to win all his fights.

After another clash went the same way, his despair hit a new low. The next morning, as he was walking through the woods, he came upon a lake and started to walk into it. A knight who represented all that was blackness and evil appeared before him in the lake and taunted him to fight. Parsifal had no more fight in him, and instead threw his sword into the water. The black knight ridiculed and taunted his insane decision, promising certain death. But Parsifal continued. He threw his shield in the lake too, followed by the heavy armor he had always worn in battle. The black knight responded with rage and mockery as this was unfolding. As the final piece of armor landed in the lake, however, the black knight dissolved and disappeared; he had been a shadowy apparition all along.

Free of his awful, heavy burden, Parsifal collapsed to his knees in gratitude and relief. In this state of openness and freedom, the mystical castle he had been searching for the whole time revealed itself before him. It had been there, right in front of him, and he hadn't seen it. As he let go of his need to defend and attack, all he had been looking for showed itself right where he was! The mystical king of this place came forward, blessing Parsifal. He truly came home the instant he let go of the need to fight.

The message in the story is very clear to me. I want to keep laying down my sword and shield more quickly every time I see that I've picked them up. This is the path to the peace that the Course promises, to keep unwinding my need to defend or attack. As I take off my armor more and more, *I* am the one who is freed.

Annihilator of Worlds

*You still have too much faith in the body as a source of
strength. What plans do you make that do not involve its
comfort or protection or enjoyment in some way?*
[Chapter 18, Section VII.I]

THE PLACID lake rested in front of me, its calm surface
reflecting the peaceful clouds drifting above. Gentle trees
and wildflowers ringed the small body of water. The bucolic scene
was the perfect spot for the healing work we were doing as a
group. This retreat was the first that I was leading by myself, and
it was going beautifully. We were very connected as a group, and
several profound shifts had already unfolded for the participants.
Little did I know that when I called for a longer break, the next big
shift would be mine.

I sat by the lake, my eyes softly closed. Fairly quickly, my
state of restfulness began to feel dark and cloudy. It felt like something big was about to show up as I went further into the cloud.
And then there it was, like a movie playing in my mind.

I could see a city. The buildings in the city were disap-
pearing; I had seen this before. Several years earlier, I visited a
chiropractor who specialized in a healing modality called Neuro

Emotional Technique. I was going through some issues with work and family, and thought that she could help. During the session, she stepped me through the technique, which was about uncovering the source of the tension or problem using muscle testing.

A number of things were surfacing and gently moving through me during the session. At times I noticed a general energetic shift, and a few times specific memories and emotions came up in order to release. One of these shifts went unexpectedly deep, and it was definitely not from this lifetime.

From a vantage point in the distance, I saw the buildings of a city. There were many large structures holding or housing thousands of people. As I watched, one at a time or in groups, the buildings blinked out of existence. They were simply gone. I knew as I watched that this was a massive attack by the enemies of our people. All the people in those buildings had just been dissolved into nothing. The super-advanced technology of the time, compared to what we have currently on our world, was being used to swiftly erase whole buildings, towns, cities. Thousands upon thousands of people were wiped out, just like that.

A terrible sense of massive loss washed over me, a tidal wave of spiritual and psychic grief. I cried while the chiropractor gently waited for these emotions to run their course. The awfulness of the scene stayed with me for a while as I worked to apply forgiveness and healing to the feelings that were surfacing. I would think about this almost unbelievable genocide off and on in the years afterwards, often feeling stunned at the inhumanity of war, no matter how 'advanced' it seemed.

And now I was seeing these same kinds of images as I meditated alongside the lake. It was the same sense of awfulness, the same sense of soul-crushing numbness, but I knew very quickly that I wasn't in the same role in this vision. This time I was the one doing it. I was the one activating the machines that annihilated whole city blocks at a time. The war machines in this vision were even larger than in the last one. They took out larger spaces of land, and consequently more people. At the high end of the scale, many millions of people were annihilated at the push of a single button — a button I pushed.

In that lifetime, for the most part, I consciously numbed myself to the intensely awful feelings that came with what I was doing. From my role up high, I didn't even really see them as people; it felt like crushing an anthill. On a soul level, however, it took a real toll. And similar to my lifetime as a bombardier, I was only implementing the commands of someone higher up. But my soul was emotionally being torn apart as I carried out the cruel and inhumane orders I was given. The guilt over putting out so many lives was a burden that weighed heavy on me, although I tried to put it out of my mind.

As I sat with the horror of killing so many people in that lifetime, more tears flowed through me. The weeping wasn't as deep or intense as I might have expected, given the awfulness of the past life that was surfacing in my mind. Why was that? The cumulative practice of forgiving the traumas and upsets in all my experiences was leading to more calmness within, even in the face of this soul-killing kind of memory. I let the tears dry and fade as this horrifying memory slowly melted.

I noticed something else about this healing. It was one of several lifetimes that made up a soul theme which could be called "Acts of Violence I Carried Out Because Someone Told Me To."

Of the lifetimes I consciously knew about, a good number fit the bill: this one, the lifetime when I nailed Jesus to the cross, my lifetime as the bombardier. They all had this same pattern, carrying out someone else's orders to injure or kill. There were other lifetimes in this pattern, wherein I had followed orders connected to genocides, crimes, and battlefield atrocities.

Now this theme was healing, releasing, being undone. We all have major soul themes activated in our lives, issues that challenge us again and again. Fully healing the karma associated with these themes allows us not to repeat the patterns later in this lifetime or any other.

As I got up from my meditation by the lake, I could tell that some major layers of the ego within me had fallen away. A generally unconscious sense of pressure and restriction was no longer in me, leading to a greater lightness and peace. What a relief, what a joy, what a blessing! As I headed back to continue leading the healing retreat, I had the amazing certainty that lots of good things were on their way.

"Trials are but lessons that you failed to learn presented once again, so where you made a faulty choice before you now can make a better one, and thus escape all pain that what you chose before has brought to you." [Chapter 31, Section VIII.3]

Karmic Categories

*Could you but realize for a single instant the power of
healing that the reflection of God, shining in you, can bring
to all the world, you could not wait to make the mirror of your
mind clean to receive the image of the holiness that heals
the world.* [Chapter 14, Section IX.7]

E ACH OF us has learning opportunities associated with certain topics that recur in lifetime after lifetime. Typical challenges include heartbreak, illness, loss of loved ones, addiction, depression, vanity, eating disorders, fears of all kinds, sleeping issues, sexual challenges, abusive relationships, chronic pain or injury, problems with money, work or career challenges, and many, many more. Such challenges show up repeatedly in different forms. Each time we are given another opportunity to undo a pattern; every repetition of the pattern is another chance to choose peace.

Another of my karmic challenges was being punished for my connection to intuitive truth. All of us have had lifetimes when we were persecuted for having 'supernatural' or unusual gifts or abilities. This is a common experience throughout many times and places, even beyond the level of burning of witches, probably the most well-known type of persecution. Many of us have also been purveyors of dark magic in some form in one or more of our incarnations. What is dark magic? Any usage of the unseen for personal gain or objectives not aligned with the highest good.

Persecution of someone with intuitive abilities clearly occurred in the lifetime when I was run out of town for trying to help someone using knowledge that wasn't common or understood, which I accessed through my intuition. Then in the lifetime as a priestess in Atlantis, I manipulated my spiritual connection for personal power and control over people who seemed useful to me in some way. Allowing these hidden or repressed past life memories to come forward was very helpful to me in undoing karmic burdens.

Other experiences fit in this karmic category. Early in my spiritual learning, I was seeing a therapist. This continued for several years after the breakdown and spiritual opening I experienced at the Landmark Forum. He was a good guy, and we talked about many things. One day I mentioned to him that I had a headache or feeling of tension in the middle of my forehead, just above my eyebrows. He mentioned that it was the position of the third eye. I didn't have much connection to that idea, even though I had heard of it before. In retrospect, I could see that the tension was associated with intuitive abilities wanting to come into the foreground of my life; I wasn't in touch with them beforehand. Karmic healing of the past often improves life in the present; I haven't had that third eye tension since.

Emerging from the Shadows

*From you can rise a world they will rejoice to look upon, and
where their hearts are glad. In you there is a vision that extends
to all of them, and covers them in gentleness and light. And in
this widening world of light the darkness that they thought was
there is pushed away, until it is but distant shadows, far away, not
long to be remembered as the sun shines them to nothingness.*
[Chapter 25, Section IV.3]

I HAVE FELT an inner pull to help people live more full and
meaningful lives for many years, at least since I started studying
massage therapy. Early in my career, I didn't have many clients, so
my healing work was sporadic even though it was something I
really wanted. I just wasn't taking all the steps I could to grow
my business. I did have several experiences that kept encouraging
me onward.

Soon after I published my first book *Questions for J – And
the Love that He Gave Me*, I was on the lookout for opportunities
to share it with the world. I had a few book signings before I
heard about an all-day workshop on "living your true passion"
that was coming to Chicago. The part that attracted me most was
the opportunity to sell my book alongside other vendors at the

entrance to the workshop hall. I was pretty green about this whole thing — I don't think I even brought a tablecloth to cover the table they gave me to use for the event! But something happened there that made a big impression on me.

One of the perks of renting a table was that I was invited to come in to the auditorium between breaks and enjoy the event itself. The speaker had a lot of good points about how to live our lives in alignment with our passion. Then she invited about ten or so volunteers to come up on stage, and I enthusiastically raised my hand. I don't remember what the particular exercise was, but I do clearly recall standing up on that stage and looking out at the audience of two hundred people. A powerful foreknowledge washed through me: in the future, I would be standing up before large groups of people who had come to hear me and experience what I had to share.

These occasional windows to what was yet to come kept me moving forward on my path. They served as the experiential breadcrumbs through the forest of my inner self. I knew they would lead me all the way home; I knew it so clearly.

A Path of Pure Non-Duality

We say "God is," and then we cease to speak, for in that
knowledge words are meaningless. There are no lips to speak
them, and no part of mind sufficiently distinct to feel that it is
now aware of something not itself. It has united with its Source.
And like its Source Itself, it merely is. [Lesson 169]

As I continue to study *A Course in Miracles*, I understand more deeply that God is real and complete Love, eternal and whole. That has always made sense to me. The part that often throws a wrench in the gears for me is the concept that *only* God is real.

I get it conceptually, but I often feel a strong aversion to this idea. A deeply held part of me doesn't really want to let go of my self. That's because there is no 'me' in Heaven. As the quote above says, there is nothing separate or apart in any way, in that state of true oneness. The ego within me perceives this as anni-hilation. Letting go into oneness seems worse than death. I do my best to practice being non-judgmental and soft when this fearful perspective arises within.

I was blessed to glimpse this nondualistic truth just a few years ago. At the time, I was working a day job in a retail setting, which seemed both good and bad. I enjoyed the people I worked with and the owners of the company were good friends of mine. However, the work wasn't very fulfilling and I would often leave at the end of the day feeling like I wasn't living the life I was supposed to. Ongoing conflict between people in my family was a concurrent challenge. Even as I was doing my best to forgive these situations and come back to the peace within, I was generally stressed about everything that was happening. It was clear to me that both situations needed healing.

Then one day I was driving home from work and experienced a sudden opening within my awareness. (I have so many stories that take place in the car, perhaps I should have titled this book *The Drive to Enlightenment!*) Feeling a bit down as I drove, and judging myself for not having my healing practice up and running, I put on a CD of a spiritual teacher to help shift me out of the way I was thinking. As I drove down the highway, the morose, self-judging energy did start reducing. Then the teacher on the CD suggested, "Ask yourself, 'What am I?'" So I did.

"What am I?" I asked within myself.

"Let me show you," came the reply from The Voice within.

What then unfolded in my awareness is a bit hard to describe. There was a seeming rip in the 'reality' of space and time. Out of that rip, or crack in space-time, poured an unbelievable amount of love, joy, peace, harmony, happiness and union. There was a sort-of light emanating from this crack that again words can't really encompass, but I'll do my best: heavenly, complete, unending, eternal, perfect holiness, beauty beyond compare... And then it dawned on me: this was an experience to show me what I truly was. I was overwhelmed and amazed! This experience was beyond anything I had conceptualized about the wonderful nature of God. And I knew it was true.

Then I had another realization: this experience, in all its wonder, was still a tiny fraction of the amazing wonder of God, and of the true Self that I was in oneness with God. Wow! I was gobsmacked with the awe of this wonderful opening. It washed over me and healed me, helping me to let go of the very concept of 'me' that I had been believing all my life.

All this unfolded while I kept driving down the highway. Tears ran down my cheeks with the beauty and amazement of it all. It was like a portal to Heaven had opened up in order to help me see the deeper truth of what I was. What a truly out-of-this-world blessing this was!

My Soul Family

My part is essential to God's plan for salvation. Just as God's Son completes his Father, so your part in it completes your Father's plan. Salvation must reverse the mad belief in separate thoughts and separate bodies, which lead separate lives and go their separate ways. One function shared by separate minds unites them in one purpose, for each one of them is equally essential to them all. [Lesson 100]

As WE travel through time and space, souls experiencing lifetime after lifetime, we find ourselves interacting with certain other souls again and again. Those whom we connect with the most often make up our soul group, or family. Often these connections are very loving and supportive, and each time we reconnect with one of these familiar souls there is a sense of celebration, even homecoming. Most of us have the experience of meeting someone and just "clicking" with them. Or we may find ourselves instantly becoming best friends with a seemingly new acquaintance. These harmonies occur when two souls reconnect in this lifetime and resume an energetic alliance as though it never ended.

There is another side to the coin, however. That is the side of ancient grudges, old wounds that haven't healed, and the bitterness of separation in various forms. On a soul level, we've done it all. We've been rich, we've been poor; we've lived in mansions and castles and extreme luxury, and we've been penniless in the ditch. We've been physically beautiful and very unattractive. Healthy, sick, successful and not, skinny and heavy, experiencing every skin tone and every form of sexuality. We've been on each side of every pair of opposites, and all over the spectrum in between.

When I consider all the different experiences my soul has been through, it makes sense that I have made some enemies along the way. It also helps explain to me why there are those people with whom I experience an immediate aversion. They are showing me the darker aspects of my soul experience. Some of those aspects are connected to lifetimes when I acted violently out of anger, and some are connected to lifetimes when I was subjected to someone's violent actions. These antagonistic connections are part of our soul group too. Darker connections represent opportunities to set down our swords and shields and find kindness and love instead. *"The holiest of all the spots on earth is where an ancient hatred has become a present love."* [Chapter 26, Section IX.6]

I have had my share of run-ins with conflicted soul connections. Some of them I have forgiven, and some I am still doing my best to let love heal. Whatever the form of conflict, the Course's technique of forgiveness is always the way through antagonism, into calm and peace.

Just as I began writing this, another soul family connection showed up. I needed to see a doctor for the first time in a couple years. When I looked at the list of available physicians, I felt strongly drawn to one in particular. We had never met before, at least in this lifetime. He was very cordial during the office visit, diagnosed my problem and prescribed some medication and course of action. There was a natural ease in our connection. After the appointment, as I was driving home, I started to feel a bit of sadness out of the blue. I acknowledged the feeling I was having, and then an ancient memory surfaced.

I knew right away that he had been my son, and died from a sickness at barely six years of age. I was devastated. He had been the warmth in my heart, and after his death it was like an inner furnace had gone out. I allowed the tears to flow as I drove down the road, feeling the rest of the despair that I just couldn't let myself move through in that past lifetime. A powerful mix of emotions arose with the mourning and, in the midst of the crying, a flash of happiness came over me. Having the chance to connect with him again was such a deep blessing. And he looked so good. His energy was solid, dependable, and he was probably supporting a family. I was so happy for his success. What a whirlwind of emotions! Happiness alternated with sadness, grief with joy. What an amazing new awareness of another member of my soul family!

Money Through the Millennia

Give up the world! But not to sacrifice. You never wanted it.
What happiness have you sought here that did not bring you pain?
What moment of content has not been bought at fearful price in
coins of suffering? Joy has no cost. [Chapter 30, Section V.9]

EVEN though I grew up in a family where money was not a problem, as an adult I've experienced inadequate cash flow. In particular, when I began pursuing my energy healing business full time, I occasionally found myself in some rough patches. My income varied from month to month, and if I had several lean months in a row, I would see my credit card balances going up. Even as I tried to practice forgiveness on this scenario, I often found it unnerving to be in this position. I wondered what the story was behind this uncomfortable dynamic.

I went to healers and some money-healing workshops in order to put the pieces together, and shift whatever unhealed issues I was having around finances. In doing so, I began to recall that I'd had experiences all over the map in this karmic category. In one lifetime, I had sold my body as a prostitute in order to survive; in another, I had been the big fat cat at the top of a lucrative business. I had been a pampered king once, and a pregnant, homeless and terrified woman in another. I had been a cut-throat businessman and a struggling trinket vendor in a street market.

A whirlwind of different beliefs about money were floating in my consciousness: *Money was dirty. Money was sinful. Having money wasn't spiritual. If I had money, then I had to be mean, otherwise people would take it from me.* This last belief seemed connected to a lifetime when I had been an upper manager in a successful manufacturing organization. We made what a certain industry needed, and we made it well. My problem in that lifetime was the feeling that people were always using me for my money. I couldn't discern who was a real friend, and who was not. It was hard, and I misread the situation at times, alienating my real friends by doubting their intentions while mistakenly trusting a few people who would end up burning me. All this turned me into a hard-edged, untrusting man who rarely if ever let people in to my life. I could afford the 'good things' in life, but it was a rather hollow victory without anyone to enjoy them with.

These beliefs had influenced the decisions I was making about money in this life. As the old perspectives were surfacing and falling away, I found myself getting more comfortable around money. I was becoming more at ease charging for my services and feeling good about it. I would always offer services affordable to most people, but I was also letting go of guilt around the price tag on my full-price offerings and feeling genuinely peaceful about it. I was amazed at what a difference it made to allow these below-the-surface beliefs to come up into the healing light of love.

One of the lifetimes that I prostituted my body was coming forward. And then I was in it:

The streets were cold, but I covered up to cope with the freezing weather. Not too much, however, because I still needed to catch the eyes of potential customers. If they didn't look, then it would mean another paltry meal of stale, molding bread that night. The best hope I had was a flash of some thigh. No properly raised woman would ever do that, but I had moved far beyond that level of decorum. My personal fall from grace had been so sudden, thinking about it felt like picking at a freshly formed scab — not a good idea, yet I found myself doing it again and again.

Larry had been a pretty miserable husband, between the excessive drinking, making passes at other women, and being lousy in bed, but he had always been able to keep food on the table and a roof over our heads. I couldn't fault him for that. When I came out of the bedroom to find him lying on the floor one morning, it just seemed natural that he had passed out after another night on the town. When he didn't move after I nudged him with my foot, a shock of horror moved through me. I bent down to turn his head, and his face had the ashen pallor that confirmed my fear. There was no life left in him at all. I fell into the corner and rocked myself in a shocked state of disbelief.

Everything fell apart quickly after that. Without any income, I lost the house and almost all our possessions. I had a little crate in which I carried the few things I had left. The little bit of money I had dried up in a few days. Then it got pretty bleak. Sleeping outside without a roof or protection from the storms was really awful. I noticed there were certain people on the streets who didn't have to sleep outside. Even though I was repulsed by the idea of selling myself sexually, the idea of continuing to live out here was even worse. When I had made up my mind, my first 'sale' happened pretty quickly. After the act, my inner shame and remorse were mostly drowned out by the certainty that I would be able to sleep in a bed that night, without the problem of my stomach grumbling so loud that it kept me from falling asleep.

Coming back from this startling recollection, the emotions of that life continued to reveal themselves to me, especially the shame of the desperate choices I had made. Later in that life, I made a vow that I would never sell myself again, no matter what my circumstances were. When we make these kinds of vows, they ring through our whole soul history and can influence dozens or even hundreds of lifetimes. This vow was still affecting me in this lifetime, in an indirect but tangible way.

One of the dynamics of starting my business was my strong dislike of asking people for money in exchange for receiving a healing. To put it another way, I didn't like selling my services in exchange for money. Eventually I saw the karmic ties that were keeping me from building my business, and could begin to let them go. Regardless of when we have made a vow, in whatever lifetime, we can only heal and release it in the present moment. In doing so, we step out of any intentional and unintentional effects of ancient decisions that no longer serve us.

EXERCISE

Dealing with Resistance

WHAT DO we do with the experience of resistance? We practice being as kind as we can with ourselves, and do our best not to fight the fear. *"[I]f you find resistance strong and dedication weak, you are not ready. Do not fight yourself."* [Chapter 30, Section I.I]

Here's the exercise:

Find a quiet place to sit for a little while. Close your eyes and go within. Take a deep breath and then another. As much as you can, let yourself witness what is going on within you. There's no need to change it. Let go of the desire to fix anything. Inwardly and quietly, just breathe and be. Let yourself take a few minutes to be here without judgment or condemnation. When the mind cranks up with a new anxiety or misgiving, let yourself be at peace with that too. When you watch the mind, you are not so wrapped up in it. When you witness your feelings, you are not controlled by your feelings. Watch it all go gently by. When it feels done, let yourself end with a thought of gratitude. Be thankful to yourself for taking the opportunity to see what's going on inside. Good job!

The Soul of a Tree

Your relationship with your brother has been uprooted
from the world of shadows, and its unholy purpose has
been safely brought through the barriers of guilt, washed
with forgiveness, and set shining and firmly rooted in the
world of light. From there it calls to you to follow the
course it took, lifted high above the darkness and
gently placed before the gates of Heaven.
[Chapter 18, Section IX.13]

A S I drove down the unfamiliar street, I felt confident that I was going in the right direction. The highway was somewhere ahead of us, and there had to be an onramp in the general vicinity. Jason and I were coming back from the retreat where we had swum in Lake Erie, and we had a truly amazing time! Driving out of the retreat center, I felt like a number of the people we'd met were part of our soul families. On the journey back to Chicago, I knew we had to pick up one of the main roads out of Erie, Pennsylvania, to get back on Interstate 90 which would take us the rest of the way back to Illinois. I didn't feel like using my phone to give me directions, so I just let my gut feeling guide us for a while. A left turn here, and a right turn at this intersection. This wasn't the way we had come in, but going this way felt right.

As I kept driving down the road, I looked to my left. One of the most beautiful maple trees I have ever seen was right there, in the front yard of a small but nice house. And I knew that I knew this tree. Instantly, with a depth that surprised me, I felt a heart-bond between me and the tree. I'd never experienced this with a tree or plant of any kind. There was a strong sense of being profoundly met and seen. All this washed over me in a matter of seconds as I slowed down the car while passing the tree.

The deep and solid connection I felt was from a past life for sure, and I realized that trees had past lives too. I had never thought about it before, but it made sense. The past life of this tree was in a different form, a bit more willowy, but still very tall. Our past life together had been in a different land, many generations ago. There was such deep love for that tree and from that tree too; I could feel it in the depth of my soul. What a gift! This 'detour' had been no accident. It was a reconnection between two kindred spirits, one in a vessel of wood, the other of flesh.

It wasn't my first rodeo with such a nature connection. Several years before this, even before the Course came into my life, I was developing my spiritual gifts in other ways, particularly through meditation. Sometimes my monkey mind would take control and I would feel very distracted as I sat for twenty to thirty minutes. Other days I would attain a much more peaceful state of being.

One day I could feel the monkey mind running wild, plus an energy of irritation and restlessness. There was a tension moving through me, but I couldn't tell what it was about. As the meditation finished I felt like going for a walk, and soon sensed that I was being nudged along. The instinct was clear: *Go left*. So I did.

Before long I saw a tree just off the sidewalk and right next to the street with a red string tied around it. Apparently a sign had hung from the string but was long gone. As the tree had grown the string had gotten tighter and was starting to cut into the bark a little. I got out my keys to cut the string with them and a sense of gratitude started to come over me. It was the tree, thanking me for helping it. The tension I had been feeling fell away then and there. I had been tuning in to the tree's painful situation during the meditation and could hear its call for help. And then I had been guided right to it. As I placed my hand on its trunk, its gratitude continued to wash over me. My own inner thankfulness welled up in response, as I was grateful to be of service in this way. The experience deepened my resolve to open myself up to being used by Spirit in whatever way was helpful.

Separation Is Not Real

The recognition of God is the recognition of yourself.
There is no separation of God and His creation.
[Chapter 8, Section V.2]

A S I continue to practice the ideas of the Course, I see its teaching come through in everything I do. In truth, there is no separation, no division of any kind. This world of time and space, however, exists in order to prove that the false is true: that separation is real.

Everything I see with my eyes seems to validate the idea of separation: people fighting one another, either individually or in groups; political parties battling for supremacy; countries attacking one another; painful issues between family members, or between families themselves; businesses fighting to get more market share. On the microscopic level, our immune systems are battling bacteria. For any body to survive, another body has to die and be consumed. Animals have to kill plants or other animals to get the energy to keep going. This world is a destructive place, where the ego's idea of "kill or be killed" rules. [Manual for Teachers, Section 17.7] The conflict, opposition, and chaos of this world goes on and on, unrolling without end like an old ticker tape machine.

Luckily for us, none of this is true. Anything that demonstrates separation, otherness, attack and condemnation, is not true. Where does it come from then? All symbols of conflict and division on the level of the world are actually projections of the ego thought system of conflict and division. This world only feels as real as it does because we have all chosen to believe that separation is real. All pain and suffering in the universe rests on this one false belief. We undo our belief in separation by healing our upsets in relation to everything that happens in our lives. By healing the anger and frustration we feel towards a specific person or situation, we begin to release our attachment to this deep, under-the-surface idea.

It always comes back to forgiveness. Again, the steps of forgiveness are:

1. *I am never upset for the reason I think.* [Lesson 5] The source of our upset is never out there, because there is no *out there*! Everything we are experiencing is happening in the mind. By remembering this, we can recall the projection of the problem from outside to within.

2. *There is no cause for upset.* On the deepest level, there is no separation. So there has been nothing that has come from separation either, in particular the world of space and time and everything it contains. Everything we experience as a body is an illusion. We cannot be upset with what is not real, if we truly comprehend that.

3. *I am determined to see things differently.* [Lesson 21] We can ask for help from Spirit in adopting a new perspective about the upset. We can learn to see through eyes of love

rather than judgment. Also, when we ask for help, it is a reminder that we are not alone.

What this really takes is practice, and we all have an abundance of opportunities. I certainly have times when it isn't hard for me to find a grievance or judgment about someone. All I have to do is turn on the TV or hop online and see what is happening in the world. I can rather easily get sucked into politics or the latest push to make the world a better place. Of course, it's never wrong to do things in the world that we think are good or helpful. But if I start using these causes as an excuse to throw away my peace of mind, I am becoming too psychologically invested in what's happening around me.

A perfect example of this is the healthcare situation in the United States. Put simply, it's a mess. Money has infected our health systems to a disturbing degree. This leads some companies to prioritize making a buck over really being of service. The healthcare system itself is sick. I remember how much I struggled with this in 2009. Barack Obama had just made history as the first African-American elected to the presidency of the United States. He made a pledge to enact universal healthcare and began taking steps to pass a massive overhaul of the US healthcare system.

I was watching all of this unfold and found myself getting swept up in the highs and lows. As the legislation began its arduous path through Congress, I would be on the edge of my seat, cheering on all the progress and getting upset by any setback. I felt upset and angry at the health insurance companies who were pushing so hard against meaningful change. I was deeply affected by all of it, and very much invested in how it all went.

This was obviously a situation that was calling for forgiveness. I could see peace instead of this — that is, if I wanted to. [Lesson 34] How to do that?

First, I spent time acknowledging my feelings, since it's never helpful to suppress emotions or thoughts. I felt like insurance companies and their allies in Congress were uncaring and unkind. Then, I remembered that I was projecting these thoughts and feelings onto the people I thought of as in the wrong. I began to ask: How was *I* uncaring and unkind? I could find uncaring and unkind thoughts in me and uncaring actions I had taken as well. Doing this inward flip alone is often helpful, since it starts to undo the feeling of victimhood.

Next, I remembered that this entire world is unreal. Since this world is a dream, I wasn't really mad at what some of the dream figures did or didn't do. I also wasn't actually mad at the dream figure of myself that I'd chosen to believe in. In reality, nothing had happened and there was no cause for upset. There was no healthcare bill with opposing forces trying to pass or defeat it. This was all a dream I had made up in order to hide from the Truth of Love because I mistakenly believed I would be punished if I came back to my Truth.

Then, I asked Holy Spirit to show me a kind way to see this situation, because I wanted to be at peace. I realized that the people who were acting out of self-interest in the healthcare fight were simply outwardly expressing the lack of love they felt on the inside. I reminded myself that all things in the world are either an expression of love or a call for love. [Chapter 12, Section I.8] When I saw their actions to defeat the healthcare bill as calls for love, I had to ask myself, "Would I deny a brother what he is asking, when he is asking for love?" The answer was no, especially when I could see that his call for love was simply a mirror of my own call for love, oneness, and peace. I would not deny him love, since to do so was actually to deny myself that very same love.

I definitely didn't do this perfectly, and found myself slipping back into victimhood, frustration, and anger quite a lot. Yet I could feel that even my irregular remembering was making a difference, simply in how I was feeling. I wasn't as upset about it as I would have been before I started working with the Course. It was a major trigger for me, but I was starting to reclaim the power I had given away to the story.

Annihilator of Worlds, Part Two

Love does not kill to save.
[Chapter 13, Introduction]

NEWS announcers were talking about it non-stop: "Stay safe during the Polar Vortex!"

"Wind chill is going to be 45 degrees below zero, so be careful when you go outside!"

"Don't go anywhere unless you absolutely have to!"

I didn't really have any plans to go anywhere since I worked from home, but I had scheduled a healing session from my friend and energy healer Melissa Matson. I was ready to email her and suggest we reschedule when something told me to hold off. As I tuned in to what wanted to happen, I felt that going to her studio for this healing session was the right thing to do. I checked in with her and she said to come on down, her place was warm and comfy.

As I expected, the healing session was profound. Current issues were unwinding as I let go of upsets and grievances I had been holding unconsciously. I did my best to allow what wanted to surface to come forward. Then something very unexpected came up.

The image in my mind's eye was familiar; I knew exactly what it was. It seemed a little silly and rather out of place, so I let it go. But it returned and persisted, I knew I had to pay attention. My mind was replaying a scene from a movie I had watched recently, *Jupiter Ascending*, made by the Wachowskis, who also created *The Matrix*. The theme of this newer film is that some people are 'harvesting' life energy from others, using it to extend their own life span and youthfulness. In my mind, I was seeing the containers that were used to store and transport life essences. In the film there were many of them, as many people had died so that one of these 'world rulers' could live a few more years until their next life force infusion.

How could this be related to my personal healing journey? Then I knew: this kind of thing actually happened in our galaxy. Certain people had used the life force of whole civilizations — whole planets of people — for their own personal life extension. They needlessly slaughtered millions of people so they could keep regenerating their physical structure, leading to a kind of twisted quasi-immortality. They were cosmic vampires on a mind-boggling scale.

I could see that in a past life I was one of them too, and then I went deeper into the memory: "Those bastards!" I raged inwardly. "They aren't going to take me down. They underestimated me before, and now look who's got the biggest empire. They're all going to rot in hell. I'll be here still, and they're going to be worm food."

I hated them so much; they were always scheming and plotting against me because they wanted the sector I owned. It was rich and full, with dozens of planets nearing manna-mining readiness. I owned so much of the stuff, stored in highly secure facilities hidden in deep space. Other than me, only my two closest advisors could access them. They wouldn't dare cross me, having witnessed first-hand the grisly deaths of their predecessors who hadn't been sufficiently loyal. Not to mention that I kept them committed to me by supplying them with a steady flow of life-renewing manna. No one else had quality as high as mine.

The others wanted my manna and would stoop to any level to get their hands on it. And they hated more than anything that a woman had outdone them. Their entreaties to partner or ally with me didn't conceal their contempt and hatred of me being their better — a woman who had thoroughly bested them. Patience was everything in this protracted game. When old age and illness ceased being factors in our lifespans, murder became the most common way for one of us to let go of our life force. But I would outlast them all! A fresh wave of rage rushed through my being as I schemed to prolong my superiority.

Experiencing that lifetime in another part of the Milky Way so many, many moons ago was intense. My narcissistic disregard for other life was so callous and uncaring, I was stunned. The agony of all those countless souls being 'processed' in this way washed through me in several waves of sadness and disbelief. As horrible as it was, I knew that in that lifetime, the massive death that I had caused seemed mundane.

Then, suddenly, I was laughing. Wow! It hadn't occurred to me when I first watched that 'fictional' movie that it was anything other than wild fantasy. And then I got it: This world is a movie too. This life in this universe is truly as unreal as any movie I have ever watched. Nothing I have ever experienced as a body in any lifetime has ever actually happened. It appears that way, but it isn't true. The truth of what I am, what all of us are, is endless, eternal love — beyond shape, form, time and space.

As my session with Melissa started to wind down, this new expansive experience kept washing over me. I was deeply moved and grateful to see that none of the shadows I had experienced had really been there at all. I hugged Melissa goodbye and headed back out into the deep freeze to make my way home.

Intuitive Guidance Within the Dream

*Your mission is very simple. You are asked to live so as
to demonstrate that you are not an ego, and I do not choose
God's channels wrongly.* [Chapter 4, Section VI.6]

A S I started on my spiritual path after college, I focused on
developing my intuition about what to do in my life. This
quickly became a useful tool. My sense of guidance led me to
know which healing workshops to participate in, and which
different healing modalities to study for certification. I used it to
figure out where to live and when to travel, and even what route
to take as I was driving somewhere.

What I didn't know at first was that I was communicating with
the Holy Spirit, as the Course would describe it. I thought of it as
tuning into my higher self, and listening for guidance from within,
doing the best I could to listen to what was in the highest good
of us all. As ACIM encourages us to ask God: *"What would You
have me do? Where would You have me go? What would You
have me say, and to whom?"* [Lesson 71] As we do this inner
asking, sometimes we will feel guidance and sometimes we won't,
but implicit in our asking is an acknowledgment that we are not
alone, and this is very important. It helps us to remember that

aloneness is a state of mind, and that states of mind can be changed.

There are some interesting questions that come to mind when we look at this guidance in light of the Course's non-dualistic teachings. For example:

"Why does it matter what we do if this whole world is only a dream?"

"Why should we do anything here in the world if nothing that happens here has any impact on the endless reality of Love?"

These are good questions, and almost everyone who studies a nondual path comes across them. ACIM students may even get depressed, or simply less motivated to do anything, as this world's unreality sinks in for them. I had some periods when I was less active in the world as I integrated these ideas. We're not left to drift hopelessly though; we are given a way through such times of indecision. When we ask to be guided in what to do in this unreal world, a deeper part of us knows that we're really asking for the fastest way back to our experience of Heaven, our divine Union with God. This is the ultimate purpose of all of our dialogue with the Holy Spirit, which we could also think of as prayer. Within the Song of Prayer supplement to ACIM, these ideas are beautifully explored:

"Prayer is a way offered by the Holy Spirit to reach God. It is not merely a question or an entreaty. It cannot succeed until you realize that it asks for nothing. How else could it serve its purpose? It is impossible to pray for idols and hope to reach God. True prayer must avoid the pitfall of asking to entreat. Ask, rather, to receive what is already given; to accept what is already there." [Song of Prayer, Section I.I]

In this paragraph, the term *idols* refers to anything specific in the world that we hope to gain, achieve, or simply experience. When we place our hope for happiness on something unfolding a certain way, we are really saying, "I will be happy *only if* ..." But a truly spiritual perspective is: *"Happiness is the essence of my being, not a state that comes and goes with changing conditions."* We will only experience the truth of this when we have relinquished all our unconscious fear and guilt over believing in the separation from God. Once again, it all comes back to practice. I know that for myself, eventually, I will persevere through it all. Love always triumphs in the end. It has to, because only love is eternal.

Epilogue

Awakening to Inner Wisdom

*You are the Kingdom of Heaven, but you have let the belief
in darkness enter your mind and so you need a new light. The
Holy Spirit is the radiance that you must let banish the idea of
darkness. His is the glory before which dissociation falls away,
and the Kingdom of Heaven breaks through into its own.
Before the separation you did not need guidance. You
knew as you will know again, but as you do not
know now.* [Chapter 5, Section II.4]

THERE IS nothing to fear in truth. At the depth of every fear
we have ever had, there is nothing there. All suffering lies on
a missing foundation. All pain is dependent on a mistaken belief
(separation) that was never true. When we pull the rug out from
under the ego, we find there was never anything there. It was all
substanceless.

This is reason to cheer! Nothing ever happened! Not really!
Perfect innocence is still our everlasting state of being! Now and
forevermore!

Let's take this attitude out with us into our days and lives.
Let's do our best to be carriers of joy and love to each and every
person, and into each massively or mildly challenging situation.

Let's make this pledge, as deeply as we can. I pledge to do this –
will you pledge this with me?

*"Father, Your way is what I choose today. Where it would
lead me do I choose to go; what it would have me do I choose
to do. Your way is certain, and the end secure. The memory
of You awaits me there. And all my sorrows end in Your
embrace, which You have promised to Your Son, who thought
mistakenly that he had wandered from the sure protection of
Your loving Arms."* [Lesson 317]

About the Author

BARRET HEDEEN has been teaching and learning *A Course in Miracles* since 2006 to help us all wake up from fear and pain into perfect peace and joy. He is an energy healer and past-life intuitive assisting others through his non-dualistic healing technique, The Witness Energy Healing. Barret leads classes and retreats around the world supporting people in letting go of their inner shadows and coming into their light.

He is the author of *Questions for J – And the Love that He Gave Me*, and *Poems for J*. Come find out more at:

www.BarretHedeen.com

His online academy for *A Course in Miracles* is a great way to dive into the Course even more deeply. Visit **www.MiraclesU.org** to start exploring!

Printed in Great Britain
by Amazon